On the River's Edge

D1332073

Centre for
Faith and Spirituality
Loughborough University

On the River's Edge

Ways into faith for waverers

PETER CORNWELL

Loughborough University & Colleges

ANGLICAN CHAPLAINCY

0085   200

Darton, Longman and Todd
London

First published 1988 by
Darton, Longman and Todd Ltd
89 Lillie Road, London SW6 1UD

© 1988 Peter Cornwell

British Library Cataloguing in Publication Data

Cornwell, Peter, *1934–*
  On the river's edge.
  1. Christianity
  I. Title
  200

  ISBN 0 232 51744 4

Phototypeset by
Input Typesetting Ltd, London SW19 8DR
Printed and bound in Great Britain by
Anchor Brendon Ltd, Tiptree, Essex

With love to all the seekers whom I have met
in Hull, Cuddesdon, Silksworth, Barnard Castle and Oxford
and who have been the real authors of this book

Contents

	Introduction	ix
1	Looking in from Outside	1
2	The Complex Package	13
3	Escape from Claustrophobia	25
4	The Holy and the Homely	42
5	The Personal Centre	61
6	The Victorious Victim	82
7	Flame in the Night	105
8	Called to the Dance	127

Introduction

Twenty-five years of ministry in the Church of England in places as varied as a Hull council estate, an Oxfordshire village, a Co. Durham mining community, a Dales market town and a university city, opened my eyes and sympathies to many who exist on the fringes of Christian faith. Unlike those who only give a rather formal nod in the direction of God on occasions of personal and national importance, these are serious about religion. They feel at once drawn and repelled by it. Looking in from outside, they are painfully conscious of not belonging and yet of their need to go on looking in. To such this book is addressed.

The first two chapters attempt to provide a frame through which the Christian 'thing' can be looked at and coped with. They are also a sort of overture hammering out themes which will be clothed with more flesh in those subsequent chapters in which I try to fit the hook of the gospel into the eye of common human experience.

One such theme is my passionate conviction that these wistful gazers-in only make progress where they are given room to make their own way at their own pace. The God and Father of our Lord Jesus Christ is the God of gentleness and patience, who woos rather than compels. If evangelism is to be Christian, and not yet one more tedious form of propaganda competing for our attention, it must conform to his ways which are frankly not our ways. It is a matter of central Christian faith that *the* mission is not our mission but that of Jesus, expressed in his living and dying, and that *our* mission can only be a share in his outgoingness which never quenches the smouldering flax but which, with infinite care, blows on it. True evangelism thus respects personal integrity and leads to freedom.

Another theme, in which I believe with equal passion, is that we seek only in order to find, and that the Christian thing, however repellent and maddening, holds before us 'unsearchable riches'. The pilgrims I have met have not embarked on their laborious journey simply for the sake of journeying. They want to get somewhere. They are thus critical, if not contemptuous and resentful, of those who, having stirred them into movement, turn round and announce 'We don't know where we are going'. While seekers appreciate efforts to meet them where they are, to connect with their experience, they feel defrauded by the offer of a faith cut to the measure of what some believers hold 'modern man' can take.

Trying to hammer out these two themes at the same time, and with equal passion, makes me fight on two fronts, against those who indulge in the 'hard sell' of a neatly packaged God and against those who seem to offer no gift but only the joys of unravelling the parcel. Pastoral experience having convinced me that neither of my opponents provides what the seeker is after, encourages me to believe that this, unlike many ecclesiastical tussles, is one worth engaging in. So, in subsequent chapters, I try to point to some paths which will take the pilgrim from where he is to where he can at least glimpse the top of a mountain which is truly beyond him and beyond us all.

I have to be frank about a problem. It seems to me that the Christian 'thing' which stands before us is something more than a series of ideas or ideals, that it is in fact a complex package of theory and action embodied in books, pictures, music, structures and imperfect human lives. This embodiment is more than a pointer to the treasure of the gospel; it actually carries it. What we are accustomed to call 'the Church', which includes but is never confined to such things as popes, bishops, priests, sacred books, solemn doctrinal statements, and forms of prayer, is in fact inescapable. This raises the very practical problem which the reader will quickly spot and perhaps complain that I have dodged. If, as I argue, this complex visible and identifiable package is all the real Christianity there is, then where is it to be found? For, when I open my front door and go in search of it, I am confronted by a number of Christian 'things', not one package but many, each claiming to be an authentic carrier of the faith. In this Christian supermarket do I just select according to taste and temperament because it does not really matter which I choose, or is only one the authentic item?

I freely admit that I have dodged this issue. For the record I have to say that I share the belief of Roman Catholics as expressed at the Second Vatican Council that this Christian 'thing', 'this Church, constituted and organised as a society in the present world, subsists in the Catholic Church, which is governed by the successors of Peter and by the Bishops in communion with him' (*Lumen Gentium*, 8). Here, I believe, is the fullest and most universal visible expression of Christianity. Readers will not therefore be surprised that I have striven to make the roads into faith roads into this particular expression of it. Anyone interested in exploring how I came thus to identify the 'mainstream' of faith can read the story in my little book *One Step Enough* (Collins Fount, 1986). However, as one who owes his faith to the nurture of the Church of England and can therefore never cease to be grateful for what God has given him through it, I embrace with equal zeal the catholic conviction, again expressed at the Second Vatican Council, both that those 'who believe in Christ and have been properly baptised are put in some, though imperfect, communion with the Catholic church' (*Unitatis Redintegratio*, 3) and that those separated from catholic unity 'whether considered as individuals or as communities and Churches . . . have been by no means deprived of significance and importance in the mystery of salvation' (ibid.). In short I recognise the scandal of competing packages of Christianity and am committed by my Church to work and pray with our common Lord: 'that they all may be one . . . that the world may believe' (John 17:21).

But I have here put to one side the task of identifying the shape and form of the Christian 'thing'. I have done this, not only because I have already written a book on the subject but also because, although it is important, it is clearly a matter of secondary importance. To identify the earthen vessel which carries the jewel of great price is necessary, but it is only necessary for the sake of getting to that jewel. Like the Greeks who came to Philip, seekers cry, not 'where is the true Church?' but, 'Sir, we would see Jesus' (John 12:21). Although I believe it to be the case that this Jesus can only be recognised in and through those patterns of believing, praying and acting which make up what we call the Church, potential pilgrims are more likely to set out on their journey if they lift up their eyes to the hills, to the goal of their seeking, rather than to the somewhat rocky terrain over which they must inevitably pass. When, as a child I began to play the piano, the first piece I learned was called 'Little Bird's First Flight'. It was not a memorable piece yet we all have to start somewhere. All I offer here are a few glimpses of the everlasting hills in the hope that the hesitating may make a start and take one or two faltering steps in the right direction.

I am grateful to Darton, Longman and Todd and, in particular, to Lesley Riddle for being so patient and encouraging as the book has slowly emerged. As usual the family and the dog have seen me through some of the bleaker moments of writing. My entry into the strange land of word processors has had its moments of agony as well as delight. A lightning flash destroyed a morning's work provoking speculation about divine intervention pursuing error from York to Hailey, and other carefully refined pages disappeared into what the handbooks assure me is Limbo. The fact that they were recovered is due to Hilary and Liza's tactful sympathy and to practical advice provided over the telephone by James and my brother Paul.

PETER CORNWELL

1

Looking in from Outside

I once knew a Co. Durham miner who, like most Co. Durham miners, never darkened the doors of his parish church save for christenings, weddings and funerals but practised some form of religion: once a year he used to go and sit quietly in Durham Cathedral. The silent massiveness of that building seemed to communicate to him something he needed. People are drawn to religion by many paths and seem to fashion different ways of relating to its institutions. Walking down the bleak cold street you glimpse the interior of a house whose curtains are not drawn. On a dark night the sight of the family gathered round the table enjoying the evening meal provides even for you, the outsider, a little oasis of warmth and light. You are not part of the family circle and would be too shy to ring the doorbell and invite yourself in, yet, as you pause, you are for a moment related to it and so helped on your journey's way. Many people are to be found looking wistfully in on the household of faith, drawn by it, envious of it, relating to it in some way and yet not feeling or even wanting to be part of it. They are glad religion with its symbols and stories is there, glad there are church buildings, pictures and music inspired by faith, even divine worship occasionally to be attended, though more often to be kept away from. 'Although I am not part of this', they might protest, 'yet I need something from it, some spin-off which moves out from the charmed circle. Indeed I have to admit that if I go to church and find the furnishings moved and the old language changed I am as disturbed as a traveller returning to find the familiar home gutted and rebuilt, the precious pictures and ornaments removed.'

1

The faith which is impossible but necessary

Iris Murdoch, in her novel *The Good Apprentice*, portrays the young man Stuart who has rejected Christian beliefs but continues in some relationship to Christianity. He ardently rejects God, his mind refusing the old story, spewing it out, 'not as a dangerous temptation but as alien tissue', and yet he feeds from the old table of faith. Stuart prays, not simply meditating but daring to make the explicit address '*Dominus et Deus*', and is engaged in a search for what, to the ears of a believer, sounds like a fine description of Christian holiness: 'He wanted to be able to be a place of peace and space to others, he wanted to be invisible, he wanted to heal people, he wanted to heal the world and to get into a situation where this would be something simple and automatic, something expected and everyday' (p. 53).

The novelist renders in fiction what Don Cupitt was feeling for in his television series *The Sea of Faith*, the sense that traditional religion is both impossible and yet necessary. For Cupitt religion now can only be 'wholly of this world, wholly human, wholly our own responsibility' (*Sea of Faith*, p. 273). 'The true God is not God as a picturesque supernatural fact, but God as our religious ideal' (ibid. p. 270). While finding the meaning of rites and ceremonies problematic, Cupitt believes they continue to be needed for their own sake. He tells the moving story of how, as a curate in the North of England, he was called out to a deathbed in the early hours of one morning:

> The patient had been quite unconscious and no relatives had come to sit by him as he died. I did not hold the magical view that giving him the last rites would actually alter his eternal destiny from what it would otherwise have been. So nobody knew I had been there and even I did not believe that I had achieved anything measurable; and yet I still thought it had been worthwhile.

In the television programme Don Cupitt went further and added that, when he came to die, he hoped he too would be a recipient of these last rites.

2

View from the bank

Here then are two writers, one a novelist and the other a theologian, who articulate a continuing need for the symbols of faith which have yet to be related to at a distance without too much commitment. They are on the river's edge, they like to see the water moving by but feel no need to jump in. Now I am bound to admit that, as a believer, I have felt the need to stand back occasionally from the Christian 'thing' and view it for a while 'at a slant'. Being something of a spectator has seemed to provide a sense of perspective difficult to achieve when you are sucked into and whirled around in the ecclesiastical flood. Even if you are off the bank and in the river, it is good to find there are a few little islands to which you can cling and so pause for a while. I have treasured those times of retreat when I could distance myself from church life while frankly continuing to draw on its resources. All this is summed up for me by sitting in the guest part of a convent chapel listening to the sisters singing the office and, while abandoning the strain and effort of joining in, allowing myself to be carried by it all. The statement of faith was being made and I was benefiting from it without being sucked into it. Recently I have had to experience this in a rather more sustained way by living, as a lay person, in the Roman Catholic Church. Of course I perform my 'religious duties' but am also able to put a certain distance between myself and a good deal of ecclesiastical life. There are difficulties in this and indeed the danger of slipping into a delightful but irresponsible escapism. However I think I begin to understand those standing on the river's edge who both need but cannot bear its waters.

If we are to get beyond testing the waters we need to be aware of the dangers which come from opposite directions, the aggression of those who would throw faith at our heads like a great slab of concrete and the well-meaning attempts of more sensitive souls who would reduce the rock of faith to clay to be moulded into a faith of our own.

3

The danger of religious aggression

Not surprisingly to the deeply committed and passionately believing, this havering on the bank seems parasitic; an indulgence in the luxury of the benefits of religion while keeping at a comfortable distance from its obligations. The complaint is like that of the party activist who does all the chores and on the day of electoral victory resents the celebrations of the party inactivists. It is the cry of the elder son who, while his brother has been living it up in a distant land, has faithfully worked at home but has never been rewarded with the feast of the fatted calf that welcomes that erring brother.

But of course the desire to hustle the hesitant springs from motives more noble than such grumbling envy. It is natural to want to share what we have found to be important for ourselves, and so hasten the outsider to the feast of faith. To such eager invitations the seeker is not unresponsive. He would love to be swept off the street to become part of that family circle, not now the outsider but the one who belongs. So he can easily be lured into making commitments for which he is not ready, swept into the household of faith, made to say he believes in things which in fact he does not. The trouble is that in being thus hustled and bounced necessary stages of his journey are bypassed. In consequence there is often a later sad awakening to the realisation that really he belongs nowhere and believes nothing. It is not surprising therefore that the cautious seeker shrinks from the loving Christian embrace. He avoids the local church and slinks into one on holiday; he lurks in the shadows of decently anonymous cathedrals. Here he is no longer crowded; he can breathe, he has the space in which to move around without his doubts and hesitations being elbowed to one side by eager believers. Here is the freedom he needs to look before he leaps.

What may look like a faithless concession to the fence-sitter is in fact an essential part of full and explicit Christian faith. If we are to see Christ standing before us in all his rugged majesty as the way, the truth and the life, making a total claim, we are also to see the Holy Spirit who abides in us as the spring which wells up to eternal life. Faith sees the Christ,

4

not as the alien intruder, but as the one who comes to 'his own', the one to whom we, made in the image of God, are fashioned to respond. At the deepest level it is natural to be a Christian for, however cluttered the internal spring may be by the rubbish of sin and triviality, it is there in every man, woman and child working to break through and bear us up to God. The basic truth is that God is on the scene of every human life and at work before any zealous Christian arrived.

If the seeker is to be helped the evangelist must learn to look before he speaks, to contemplate this quiet mysterious presence of God, so that instead of lobbing in the gospel from outside he first learns to adore the Spirit who 'searches the hearts of men' (Rom. 8:27) and then be content to be that Spirit's modest assistant. The individual has to be drawn out of the crowd, and the drama of his unique journey discerned. This means that the temptation to hustle the seeker into the garments of faith must be resisted. David was called to go out against the giant Goliath and King Saul offered him his own armour for the encounter but David was ill at ease in it and had to choose his own weapon, the sling and smooth pebble. The pilgrim encounters many Sauls eager to squeeze him into the whole armour of God. In a way these Sauls are right. What could be better than this armour? How could anything less than the full riches of God be offered? The trouble is that unless integrity is respected and the particular path to God for this individual discerned, these riches cease to be a gift and become a heavy burden. 'The truth' becomes a stick with which all too real questions and doubts are beaten out of us. When John Henry Newman spoke of 'the principle of reserve' in communicating religious knowledge, he was not making concessions to British tight-lipped embarrassment at the mention of God, but insisting both on care in bearing witness to the overwhelmingness of God and sensitivity towards the needs of the pilgrim. None knew better than he how religious aggression could cheapen faith and set back the seeker.

The danger of reducing the banquet of faith

However this insistence on literally divine patience, which allows us, at our own pace, to taste and see how gracious the Lord is, must not be confused with a move to reduce the banquet to a mere snack. There are those who claim that the problem is not that the hungry are forced to gobble the meal of faith but that the meal itself is indigestible to modern stomachs. Instead of adjusting the pace of eating we should, more radically, turn from the flab-fashioning myth and dogma of former ages to the low protein and bran diet suitable for the twentieth century. 'We do not these days pray for light but turn to the switch in the sure and certain hope that light will come. We have no need of the supernatural. If you are drawn to the teachings of Jesus but cannot make sense of God, then abandon the notion of God as an objective reality but retain the word as a label you can attach to those ideals you have drawn from Jesus. The label will proclaim the seriousness of your commitment to them. You cannot make much of the Church with its creeds and dogmas but you may still recognise that even in religion "no man is an island" and are able to see that its institutions provide the necessary framework of rituals and stories which can stimulate you in fashioning a faith of your own'.

This is in fact very different from the appeal to go quietly and gently in our journey into faith. Here faith has, in Don Cupitt's words, become a matter 'of working out our own personal vision of God' (*Sea of Faith*, p. 271). In this the community's tradition of faith may help but the goal is, quite clearly, the fashioning of my own 'autonomous faith'. Traditional faith, in contrast, while insisting that 'the faith of the Church' should become 'my faith', not just a slab of ideology acquired but fully personal, yet insists that this comes not through autonomy but through belonging and interdependence. Instead of aspiring to a 'faith of my own' I am led to share in a common faith and am thus lifted out of the shallow puddle of my own ideas to be enriched in a world of wider experience.

In fact the desire for autonomous religion looks something like the once fashionable educational theory of single-minded 'child-centredness', which suggests that all knowledge lies within the individual and waits only to be tapped. Education is there, it was claimed, not to impart information but to draw out what lies locked within the child. The school exists to provide a framework in which children discover their own resources of truth. Of course there is insight in this and, religiously, it connects with our insistence on the uniqueness of each individual's path to God, but by itself it is an unbalanced insight. In the language of faith one could say that the 'immanence' of truth, the light within, has not been balanced by 'transcendence', the truth which towers over us requiring our total obedience. In seeking the truth our task is not to squash reality into the pint-pot of our apprehension, but to let those pint-pots be stretched, smashed and refashioned to fit reality. This is not slavery but freedom; freedom from being locked within ourselves, a freedom offered not only in formal education but in crafts, hobbies and skills, which, as we say, 'take us out of ourselves'. Reality is not locked up in our tiny heads, it is outside us and we grow in knowledge by engaging in the hard and often wearisome business of wrestling with it and being stretched by it. All our fine ideas and theories have to bend the knee to the facts of the matter; our absolute obligation is to conform ourselves to what is true.

The trouble with Cupitt's autonomous 'working out my own personal vision of God' is that it looks as if it must inevitably end with a self-made 'god' tailored to the measure of my mind, a religion which is really nothing more than the icing on the cake that is already there. As such it is obviously vulnerable to the accusation that here is nothing more than a projection on to the skies of my deep-down desires and longings. What is this product but what our critics have always said it is, an ideology brewed to justify the present ordering of things, whether that be my personal life or the form of society in which I have a vested interest? Autonomous religion thus looks not radical but deeply conservative.

But is not the one poised on the river's edge looking for something more than his reflection in the waters; does he not look for something beyond what his present experience has to offer? However much traditional faith may puzzle or repel, the seeker does not want it to lose its shape and identity and become simply clay to be moulded to his needs. While surprisingly modern men and women look wistfully at solid and confident expressions of belief, they seem to lose all interest when confronted by it in its more pliant and accommodating forms. One has heard critics of the obscurantism of orthodoxy reserve their fiercest scorn for well-intentioned clerics and theologians who are striving to meet their objections. Although this is maddeningly perverse it does seem to express an instinctive feeling that religion is most helpful when it has the inner self-confidence not to be for ever looking over its shoulder, worrying about what the neighbours think, but gets on with the business of being itself.

This does not mean that religion should float above the problems and questions of a particular age pretending phoney timelessness. There are lessons to be learnt from the creative artist. He will only successfully communicate if he is truly present in his age, immersed in its agonies and hopes, a genuine child of his time; but equally only if he preserves some detachment and ceases to worry about what the public will make of his work. There in our midst he dreams dreams and sees visions. It is enough for him to be faithful to these dreams and visions. He must say what he has to say whether they hear or forbear to hear. A recent radio discussion between composers made this point. They longed for their music to get through and make sense to everybody and yet when they composed they had to shut out the world and renounce any striving for popularity. Peter Brook, in his work on the theatre, *The Empty Space*, well expresses this attachment with detachment, this sensitivity and indifference: 'The actor's work is never for an audience, yet always is for one. The onlooker is a partner who must be forgotten and still constantly kept in mind; a gesture is a statement, expression, communication and a private manifestation of loneliness' (p. 57).

So if faith is to communicate it has to show the pilgrim that there are paths which open from where he is, but equally that these paths will take him somewhere he has never been before. The fell-walker will not embark upon the most enticing mountain without some map which shows he can get from where he is to where he wants to go, but equally he is unlikely to move out of bed on a cold wet morning if all he is offered is a tame excursion up a grassy mound. The pilgrim wants to know the journey is possible but he wants an adventure into the unknown.

Taking Christianity as it is – complex and visible

But what is this mountain which looms out of the mist and is said to offer such promise? The bit most obvious and newsworthy seems all a matter of popes and bishops, of clergymen and synods. If that does not seem a very promising start for the pilgrim he may turn instead to that bit which is to hand in the local church or chapel. This may prove equally unappetising and he may prefer to skirt the peat bogs of institutional religion and make for the Bible or other writings of this verbally prolific organisation. But the way of words, words, endless words may seem an equally stony path. What looks more promising is faith in action, that way of life exemplified in the saints. The truth is that the Christian thing is all this. It is not monochrome, reducible to some simple essence but a complex, multidimensional enterprise woven out of the institutional, intellectual and experiential. It is as much old ladies lighting candles and praying as bishops laying down the law; as much artists painting and musicians composing as priests at the altar; as much Mrs Jones and Mr Smith struggling to be good neighbours as evangelists thundering to the thousands; as much the politician working for justice and peace as the theologian's contribution to a learned journal. If you try to distil out of this rich mixture something simple and essential you will end up not with Christianity but with a piece of paper, a merely notional religion.

As so complex a visible thing and not just a bloodless ideal, Christianity is set before us like a picture in an art gallery. This picture exists to reveal the 'picture' of Jesus who in turn is called the picture or 'image' of the invisible God (Col. 1:15). But there is a problem. The analogy of Christianity as a picture suggests a work of art with an unchanging face. Once the picture is painted there it hangs in the gallery,

9

indeed to be viewed from different angles but in itself complete.

Change and continuity

You could say that the unchanging portrait is precisely what we are looking for in religion, that fixed secure point amidst the flux of an ever-changing world. While 'time like an ever-rolling stream bears all its sons away', we turn to the mystery which is not the victim of time, the point of stability, 'our shelter from the stormy blast and our eternal home'. This is a sure and proper instinct yet it has to be recognised that the face of the Christian thing is inescapably marked by time and we only deceive ourselves when we use old-fashionedness as a symbol of timelessness.

We talk about the 'unchanging' Latin mass or Book of Common Prayer, and see the King James Bible, old hymns, the way things were done when we were young, the screen in its place in church and the altar firmly against the east wall, as symbols of the very permanence and eternity of God. Yet our mind tells us there is no security to be found here. The old hymns were mostly nineteenth-century upstarts, the history of liturgy is the history of constant evolution and that all too solid screen is probably not more than a hundred years old. I know people for whom church music without an organ is unthinkable, who are oblivious of past battles to prevent the imperialist organ driving out the local orchestra. You only have to read Thomas Hardy's *Under the Greenwood Tree*, where for the old villagers not the organ but 'strings is soul music', to see how precarious the established and customary ways are as symbols of timelessness. In truth old English parish churches reveal not the unchanging but layer upon layer of change. In one generation statues are removed, in another pews are added. Sometimes the changes simply register taste or religious emphasis but at other times they articulate fundamental alterations in the understanding of faith and society. At Rycote Chapel near Thame you will see in architectural form something of what the English Reformation involved. Gone is the rood screen with its crucifix and in its place is the royal coat of arms. Now the towering two-decker pulpit dwarfs the modest communion table while luxurious private pews for the gentry contrast with the bare benches provided for the lower orders. What is true of the signs and symbols of faith is, as we shall see, true of its verbal expressions. Doctrines do not drop from heaven, even the Bible does not drop from heaven, both have to bear their witness in an ever-changing world from which the language of faith cannot be insulated. In the New Testament we can trace ideas being hammered into new shape and we find ourselves having to speak of the development of doctrine.

Would it then be better to say that this complex Christian bundle is a picture in the 'process' of being painted, that the image it claims to show of Christ is an image slowly emerging? Yet this would be to make 'revelation', the unveiling of the image, imply that the later we come in on the action the more we should be able to see; that twentieth-century Christians are thus better off than first-century ones. But this does less than justice to the community's insistence on the given 'once-for-allness' of faith which has been consistently expressed by checking new developments by the authoritative articulation of that givenness in scripture. The community has worked on the principle that the divine artist made his definitive statement in the living, dying and rising of Jesus as witnessed by his closest friends, and that what follows is not addition by the painter but the possibility of ever deeper understanding by the viewer. The Christian tradition of pondering does not add to the portrait a few finishing touches but is more like the pondering of the art critic enabling us to grasp more fully what has been given and encouraging us to view the portrait from fresh angles and thus to acquire further insight.

Perhaps this theme of development and continuity is better seen from the analogy of the drama. Here there is one script, which is the enduring thing; we do not rewrite the plays of Shakespeare. Elizabethan and twentieth-century theatregoers really do experience the same drama. But that which endures exists to be again and again reenacted in ever fresh productions. Faithfulness to the script requires not imitation of the past but new interpretations. 'Deadliness in the theatre', writes Peter Brook, 'always brings us back to repetition, the deadly director uses old formulae, old methods, old jokes, old effects, stock beginnings to scenes, stock ends' (*The Empty Space*, p. 44). But Brook distinguishes this need for new productions with fresh understandings from a gimmicky modernism which has lost faith in the writer's intention and has cut loose from his script. Life 'is moving, yet a great theatre is not a fashion house; perpetual elements do recur and certain fundamental issues underlie all dramatic activity' (ibid. p. 19).

2

The Complex Package

If we begin to see Christianity not as an ideal theory but a complex package, we shall be attending to the real thing. However this 'reality' repels as well as fascinates. It has blood on its hands and contains as much pride, cruelty and self-seeking as any secular movement. The sins of organised religion are peculiarly repulsive for here familiar evil is masked by a veneer of piety or justified in the name of God. No wonder reformers are tempted to break up the package and start again with some spiritual kernel extracted from this unattractive shell. Who, faced with yet fresh evidence of ecclesiastical awfulness, has not felt the urge to lay into the monstrous old temple with axes and hammers, crying, 'Down with it, down with it, down to the ground'? No distortion of the truth is so terrible as those bland rewritings of the past which seek to smoothe away the warts from the face of Christendom.

The illusion of pure Christianity

However if the 'real thing' with its all too grubby past is sobering, attempts to scrap it and start all over again with a pure and disinfected Christianity are disappointing. The old pope may be driven away but then you find that you have spawned many little popes who are no longer safely tucked away in Italy but on your doorstep in the local parish church. The idols of wood and stone may have been smashed but new ones fashioned from words and ideas emerge and prove to be more subtle adversaries. Somehow the purer you try to be and the more determined you are to cast off the flesh of old institutions, the greater the fall is, the more you become

13

enmeshed in self-deception. I once knew a Christian community which prided itself on dispensing with all hierarchical forms and without priest or minister tried to live as simple brothers and sisters in Christ. The truth was that one brother and his family were more equal than others and in fact ruled the community with a rod of iron.

All this is not very surprising for Christians have always believed that the deadliest danger does not come from the flesh but from the illusion that, escaping from the flesh, you can escape sin itself. In biblical terms it is when Adam is not content to be a flesh and blood human and aspires to be 'as God' that he falls. The church of 'the pure' ruthlessly cutting away second-rate citizens and providing only a prize for saints or 'real' Christians, does not in fact scale the heights but plunges into the depths to become an instrument of pride. Where the goal is seen as a pedestal on which a small élite can clamber, away from their grubby, sensual, ordinary brothers and sisters, there true faith is denied. 'He who does not love his brother whom he has seen cannot love God whom he has not seen' (1 John 4:20).

I do not underestimate the dirt which clings to the Christian thing but I insist that a fastidious dodging of dirt leads not to sanctity but to sin. Peter Brook shows how great dramatists incorporate the 'rough' as well as 'the holy': 'If we find that dung is a good fertiliser, it is no good being squeamish; if the theatre seems to need a certain crude element, this must be accepted as part of its natural soil' (*The Empty Space*, p. 74). He goes on to give a fascinating illustration of this inclusion of 'dirt':

At the beginning of electronic music, some German studios claimed that they could make every sound that a natural instrument could make – only better. Then they discovered that all their sounds were marked by a certain uniform sterility. So they analysed the sound made by clarinets, flutes, violins and found that each note contained a remarkably high proportion of plain noise, actual scraping, or the mixture of heavy breathing with wind on wood; from a purist point of view this was just dirt, but the composers soon found themselves compelled to make synthetic dirt, to 'humanise' their compositions. (ibid.)

The same seems true of religion. Spiritual squeamishness, the rejection of the dirt which mingles with the glory, produces a sterile dehumanised and unreal faith.

New clothes for old faith?

Perhaps we are not saying that any real religion can exist as a kernel plucked from its shell but that a new and better shell can take the place of what is unsatisfactory or simply dated. Granted the gospel's need for clothing, why not exchange the old clothing for new? If we go on heaping new clothes over the old, Christianity will become overdressed and we shall no longer see the shape and form within. It becomes the work of art no longer illuminated but obscured by the verbosity of commentators.

Christian renewal certainly involves an element of pruning, of cutting back over-luxuriant growth so that the shape of the tree can be rediscovered and the portrait of Christ 'the image of the invisible God' recovered. But in this struggle to see the wood for the trees the community of faith does not jettison its past. It needs to claim continuity with that past in a practical and visible way, to declare its solidarity with the faith of a Paul, Augustine, Cuthbert or Aquinas. However curious their understandings of faith may seem to us, however deep the gulf between their age and ours, yet we wish to claim them as fellow believers. This is our past to be accepted and loved. The family photos of grandparents and great aunts may show strange fashions but we treasure them, for after all we are part of them, chips off these old blocks. This is not just sentiment. We may find things in our past that we unexpectedly need to reclaim. Ruthlessly tidy people throw away their junk, hoarders stack it in the attic for they never know when that old top hat or cardboard box may not come in useful. Junk has an odd way of becoming treasure. So instead of scrapping funny old bits of its past the Christian community stores it up for a rainy day. Its developing life is not ever upwards and onwards to greater perfection; new insights in one area may be accompanied by amnesia in another. If the community's attic looks like a jumble sale, that may be because it knows the past has its insights which one day may possess a new relevance we want to reclaim.

The demands of the real thing

Instead then of extracting some pure essence of faith or dressing it up in the trendiest fashion, there seems to be wisdom in taking it as it is with all its burdens and treasures of the past. It is surely better to be bewildered and even scandalised by what is real than to fly to some blueprint which has never got off the drawing board. Of course this, like all reality, is more demanding and puzzling than some misty ideal. Some art seems to offer instant delight but great works require careful and sustained attention. Who has any respect for the casual wanderer through the art gallery muttering obstinately that he 'knows what he likes', refusing even to consider what goes beyond the narrow limits of his appreciation? The humble seeker who wants to have his eyes opened to beauty beyond his imagining knows that he must stand still, consider carefully and wrestle with what puzzles or even repels. Works of art yield up their treasures to those ready to give time and attention. To listen again and again to one piece of music is to discover ever new depths in it. It is not otherwise with faith. It offers no instant delight, but treasure to those who seek, knock and ask. The dismissive 'that I cannot believe' is the equivalent of the philistine's 'I know what I like'.

After all it is this confused and confusing enterprise which in fact carried and still carries the gospel treasure. There is no escape from it. Even if you go into solitude to read the Bible and extract from it some simple faith of your own, the truth is that you will still be dependent on the labours of those who wrote these occasional pieces and others who collected and preserved them. Nothing illustrates this more impressively than the fact that the writings of the Old Testament prophets, those fiercest critics of the ecclesiastical enterprise, were treasured and handed on to us by their very victims the priests, the guardians of that enterprise. Radical critics and agents of reform are formed and carried by the very body they judge and seek to change. Of course prophets always get a better press than priests for they bring fire and excitement while dull ecclesiastics seem to reduce faith to formal routine. I have wandered into a village church on a Sunday evening and with its handful of elderly ladies, wheezing organ and tired grey clergyman, have not found it an inspiring occasion. Yet within that village this is the reality which continues to hand on the faith, to keep the rumour of God alive. Perhaps one day men and women will arise to put flesh on these bare bones, and that will be good, yet less good if they forget the rock from which they have been hewn.

This funny mixture is all the real Christianity there is, but in accepting it as it is I am not just making the best of a bad job, accepting a dire necessity. By being confronted with something objective I am rescued from dreams. I find I am at least looking beyond myself. What I see may be puzzling or even repulsive but at least I can be sure that this is not the religion I would have fashioned for myself. To attend to forms of worship which seem bizarre, to ways of thinking which seem outlandish, to styles of life which seem extravagant, reminds me that my mind is not the measure of all things. I am being invited to explore areas into which I have never dared venture. The faith I would like, the church of my choosing, would in truth offer only a safari in my vegetable garden. Although I might seize my shotgun and wear my topee it could never become a real jungle. Take the Christian thing as it is, then I really am in a jungle with the possibility of unexpected beasts round the corner.

Seeing is believing

I have deliberately been talking about the Christian thing as a picture to be looked at or a drama to be watched rather than a message to be listened to. This emphasis on its visual nature may at first seem puzzling. We are eager to hear what faith's message is, to study its manifesto. Did not St Paul insist that faith comes from what is preached, and what is preached comes from the word of Christ (Rom. 10:17), while 'seeing' seems reserved for heaven (1 Cor. 13:12)? In fact for the Bible the word to be heard and the image to be seen belong closely together. Its writers do not speak of God in abstract language but in a whole riot of images: God the shepherd, king, husband, rock, fire, and so on. Indeed the Old Testament tells a story rather than proclaims a message. In a whole series of very human dramas God is pointed to as the mysterious unseen central character. Jesus, by calling not only for ears to hear but also for eyes to see, continues in this tradition. When he teaches he does not make flat dogmatic statements but tells stories which conjure before our eyes homely scenes of ordinary life. Christians see in the life story of Jesus more than the offer of noble teaching, they recognise it as the very 'story' of God. His intimate friends are more than hearers of the word, they are 'eyewitnesses of his majesty' (2 Pet. 1:16). The priority of this 'seeing' is kept alive in the Christian tradition of prayer which encourages us to move through words and ideas to rest content in contemplating the Lord. It is 'through beholding the glory of the Lord', says St Paul, that we ourselves are 'changed from one degree of glory to another' (2 Cor. 3:18–4:6). This is to have a foretaste of that journey's end which is nothing less than the vision of God, when 'we shall see him as he is'.

The appeal to the imagination

The invitation to 'come and see' means that faith addresses the imagination before the mind. It can argue its case, give explanations of a wearisome length, and yet, when it comes to persuasion, the crib, the cross, the liturgy, the holy life, reach parts of us where no argument can go. These work on our imagination like works of art eliciting from us a real assent. 'This', we say, 'makes sense to us. It points to what is supremely worthwhile.' We shall see later that this constitutes no escape into irrationalism. However it does mean that faith addresses a circle wider than those who can follow arguments or give a ready ear to explanations. Faith, by speaking to the imagination, is accessible to all. The only expertise it requires is that of experts in the imagination, children.

The reason why such an appeal suggests the imaginary, in

the sense of the illusory, is that we suffer from an unreasonably low doctrine of the imagination. While we take 'reason' to deal with 'hard' truth we treat the imagination as a non-essential luxury, a flourish or adornment on the solid house of serious living. While the white-coated scientist is believed to deal with 'fact' the long-haired emotional artist is held to be mildly unbalanced. Yet G. K. Chesterton was right when he insisted that it was not imagination which bred insanity. 'Exactly what does breed insanity is Reason' (*Orthodoxy*, p. 25). 'The madman is not the man who has lost his reason. The madman is the man who has lost everything except his reason. The madman's explanation is always complete and often in a purely rational sense satisfactory' (ibid. p. 30). The only trouble, and it is fatal, is that his neat coherent explanation bears no relationship to reality. On the other hand, as practising scientists are ready to admit, in the search for the real it is often the imagination which leaps forward to grasp it, while reason limps somewhat behind.

Advertisers understand the power of the imagination. They do not persuade us of the superiority of a soap powder by chemical analysis but through images of 'the good life', which speak to levels in us deeper than our minds. In the art of political persuasion the imagination also takes the lead. People do not vote for a party because they have read and weighed the party manifestos and have decided that the arguments of one are better than its rivals. Normally votes are won by how a party is seen, by a complex package made up of the personality of the leader and a bundle of impressions, that this party is more in touch with the needs of ordinary folk or that party offers greater rewards to the successful and enterprising. The party 'image' is projected and imaginations are caught by this image. One could say of effective political communicators what Wilfrid Ward said of Newman, that they 'favour massive reasons that influence the whole man. They are suspicious of clear arguments that appeal only to logical acuteness' (W. Ward, *Last Lectures*, p. 35).

It is not otherwise with the appeal of the practical secularism whereby most members of our society live. Of course its articles of faith can be spelt out. Life has no overall meaning: it is bounded by the inevitability both of the death of individuals and, in the end, the death of our universe. Between what Bertrand Russell called these 'twin pillars of despair' we take up our human task, which is to fashion oases of meaning and value, work out our own way of making life worthwhile. Most of our contemporaries in the West have adopted such a belief system yet they have been so 'converted' not because they have sifted arguments or weighed scientific evidence, but again because their imaginations have been captured. Secularism also has presented its image, offered an overall impression: 'Science works and has delivered the goods of a more comfortable life, and because science deals only with the visible tangible world this world is the only reality. To accept this is liberty, for if I can shake off the myth of some overall meaning to life I am set free to choose for myself which of the good things science has to offer I shall take. In the most radical way I become the architect of my own destiny.' Something like that is the 'faith' by which our society lives. That is the image of secularism which has got across and has produced its converts. While argumentation may have won the few, this appeal to the imagination has reached the many.

The continuing claims of the reason

But if imagination thus leads the way in the business of persuasion, that does not mean that it can be cut free from the claims of reason. The thoughtful secularist knows that his faith system must be shown to be not only attractive but true. However much quiet reasoning may go to the wall during an election campaign, the serious politician knows that the party image has to be rooted in cogent argument. Though few may read the manifesto, yet it has to be there to be scrutinised and rationally defended. Where politics descend into the mere pursuit of successful public relations there ascends the all too familiar smell of corruption. The heart is deceitful. The imagination can be captured by illusion and nightmare for it is an eager receiver able all too easily to lap up lies as well as truth. Recently I came across a copy of Hitler's *Mein Kampf.* Although I read only a few pages I began to understand how sensible people could be drugged by the heady vision of this skilled communicator. I had to shake myself to wake up to the fact that the vision was one of abysmal wickedness.

Battered by the alluring images with which 'the hidden persuaders' probe our imaginations, our critical reasoning faculties need to be ever sharper. In fact it is rationality which is under threat. There is some disillusionment with the white-coated omniscient scientist and thus a temptation to thrust the very reason we once elevated into a deity into the depths as a devil. There are signs of retreat from rationalism into mindless hedonism or unbridled fantasy. Old cultures and religions of the East have woken to realise that western secularism threatens to erode their distinctive ways of life and they are responding with a fundamentalist reassertion of identity. In the West too, modern man is to be found embracing simplistic forms of Christianity or retreating into the strange byways of bizarre cults. The frustrated imagination seems to be running riot seeking escape from a world which has become both impossibly complicated and deprived of all sense of meaning and purpose. Chesterton was right to recognise that the very age of rationalism which had scorned the imagination was beneath the surface an age 'at war with reason' (*Orthodoxy*, p. 55).

Authentic Christianity has never dodged the question 'is it true?' It has always held that imagination and mind should walk together. The careful reasonableness of a Thomas Aquinas is as much a part of its complex package as its organisation, its liturgies and its art. All those wearisome books, all the laboured argument against obscure deviations, which seem so nit-picking and arid, at least indicate that this is a body concerned with more than wild visions and emotional thrills. So-called proofs of the existence of God may leave us cold, yet it is not without significance that they go on being mounted and indeed taken seriously by unbelieving philosophers to the extent that they continue to write books to demolish them. This intellectual activity shows that Christianity will not rest content with God as a beautiful idea, that it must stake all on his being real. If God is not real then Christianity is untrue and we ought not to believe in it. It is this serious central issue of truth which the trimmers of faith have blunted. Having conceded that the secularist is right to deny the objective reality of God, the trimmer is content to commend the ethics and spirituality of the old faith. This salvaging of treasure from the wrecked hulk may show admirable sentiment and even sound conservationist zeal, but it makes faith ultimately immune from the question 'is it true?'

Reasoning for all

But if we insist that the imagination cannot be set free from the claims of the mind, do we not make honest faith possible only for an intellectual élite? Having said that through its appeal to the imagination faith is available to all sorts and conditions of people, we seem now to be making it a more specialist affair. To put it bluntly it looks as if the Christian enterprise has to be exposed to literary critics who will scrutinise its foundation documents, to historians who can say in principle what probably happened in Palestine all those years ago, and to philosphers who will probe whether the language of faith is sense or nonsense. If faith submits to the testing of reason then it submits to a highly technical operation. What can the man on the Clapham omnibus do? Will he sign on for evening classes to acquire these intellectual skills or make an act of faith in what the experts tell him? While the first course may be impossible the second is surely passing the buck of a personal task to a set of outsiders. Indeed these outsiders, being scholars, are an argumentative lot and it will not be clear whose judgement we should follow.

Better far that the man on the Clapham omnibus should take his courage in his hands and insist on doing his own amateurish job. For if, as we have said, the role of the imagination has been devalued, that of the mind has become overspecialised, turned into an arcane and élite activity, snatched from the people and put into the hands of experts. Let me illustrate this. People's reaction to terrible moral challenges, such as reliance on the nuclear deterrent or the destruction of unborn children, is often a 'gut reaction' – 'This is wrong! This is evil!' Such simple directness is rebuked as naive. No sound moral judgement can be made on these matters, it is argued, where complexity has been ignored. Not surprisingly ordinary people begin to lose confidence in their capacity to say what is right or wrong. Perhaps all moral judgements have now become a matter for experts and the likes of us are let off the hook of personal judgement and responsibility. It is one greatness of Newman that he resisted this specialisation of reason. He recognised that faith does not come to us through the reason: 'If children, if the poor, if the busy can have true faith yet cannot weigh evidence, evidence is not the simple foundation on which faith is built' (*University Sermons*, p. 231). Yet he is deeply opposed to the notion of the 'simple faithful' as lumpenproletariat incapable of reason. 'Reason is a living spontaneous energy within us, not an art' (ibid. p. 257). In fact we are all more reasonable than we think we are. 'All men reason but all men do not reflect upon their reasoning. All men have a reason, but all men cannot give a reason.' Instead of pushing the responsibility of being reasonable on to experts we need to recapture confidence in our native wit, to affirm that common sense really is sense.

The man on the Clapham omnibus is capable of practical judgement. He blends sensible trust with proper scepticism. He has confidence in the general trustworthiness of his senses. He has no doubt that he exists and is in the bus. He knows his faculties are generally trustworthy and thus calls a spade a spade. Of course he knows there is room for error, that what seems a spade in the darkened garden shed may turn out to be a hoe, but such mistakes do not undermine his sensible trust. Though he is reasonable he distrusts those rationalists who seem to try to fit all life into a neat filing system. Real life is not like that, it is far too big to be easily weighed, measured and encapsulated. There is a disorderliness to reality which eludes classification on the official form. The anarchist in us rejoices when the unexpected pops up through the surface orderliness of things to upset the expectations of experts.

This native wit with its blend of trust in reality, and scepticism about drawing limits to that reality, is sufficient equipment with which to test that image of faith that is presented to our imaginations. While it would be ill at ease distilling some pure essence of religion, it can take things as they are. If it is religion that is to be considered, such practical reason will head first not for the library but for the church or chapel down the road. That is real and solid, as is the priest with dandruff and a squint, as is the churchwarden who takes the collection on Sundays and sells sprouts on Mondays. Here is something to be coped with and attended to and native wit with its resources of good humour and quiet scepticism is able to sift out the folly and pretence. It knows the genuine article when it sees it and is well equipped to answer the question, 'Does this rickety signpost point to a dead end of illusion or to those heights and depths which we know to be part of the rich tapestry of life?'

3

Escape from Claustrophobia

The religion which points to but does not capture mystery

If we returned to that miner sitting alone in Durham Cathedral and asked him what exactly he was doing, he would have difficulty in giving a clear answer. He was just being there, gazing up into the vastness, allowing himself to be overwhelmed by space and silence. For many people faith is best when it ceases to be 'poor talkative Christianity' and has the confidence to lead us into silence. It offers words which have power to evoke, music which leads to that gasp of wonderment before the applause breaks out, architecture which sends the eye away into darkness. I have heard children complain that many modern churches are so uncompromisingly open and bright that there are no places to hide in. They say they prefer churches with dark niches and shadows where a warmer and more modest light breaks through the stained glass windows or struggles up from flickering candles. We do not want our religion to hold down and encase mystery, but to point beyond itself. E. M. Forster gets the feel of this in his *Passage to India*, when he writes:

> Mrs Moore found God increasingly difficult to avoid as she grew older, and he had been constantly in her thoughts since she entered India, though oddly enough he satisfied her less. She must needs pronounce his name frequently, as the greatest she knew, yet she had never found it less efficacious. Outside the arch seemed always an arch, beyond the remotest echo a silence. (p. 52)

What makes us pay attention?

To claim that we live in a pluralistic world is to acknowledge that we are no longer confronted by one official system of beliefs and values but that many compete for our attention and allegiance. We are wandering through an art gallery with a bewildering multiplicity of pictures, a supermarket which offers far more than the old cornershop's limited range of goods. Variety may be the spice of life but it makes us restless viewers and desultory pickers and choosers; we stop to look only when something has immediate appeal. Clearly this makes it difficult for Christianity as a complex and demanding work of art to claim our attention. Often we are only halted in our tracks and made to reflect by some event which shakes and changes the direction of our lives. Marriage, the birth of a child, a mid-career crisis, bereavement; these are often the occasions, joyful or devastating, which make us take stock and allow faith a hearing. Let us be honest: sometimes it is plain disillusionment. Pleasures have become dulled and more or new pleasures only bring nausea; personal ambitions have not been fulfilled and we have to face the fact that now they never will be; the political party to which we have given our allegiance has not delivered the new Jerusalem it promised. Life has not lived up to our expectations and we sense the emptiness of those glittering prizes it still holds out to us:

> We are the hollow men
> We are the stuffed men
> Leaning together
> Headpiece filled with straw. Alas!
> Our dried voices, when
> We whisper together
> Are quiet and meaningless
> As wind in dry grass
> Or rats' feet over broken glass
> In our dry cellar.
> (T. S. Eliot, 'The Hollow Men.')

To admit so frankly that it is often disillusionment which makes us pay attention to faith seems to be giving the game away. Is this not what critics have always said, that religion is opium, an alternative to drugs or drink, called on to ease the pain of 'the dead land – the cactus land'? But this is to give 'disillusionment' a bad name. In itself it is something positive, the shedding of illusion and the clearing away of false dreams, the necessary prelude to awakening to reality. Far from providing a lying distraction for those who cannot bear too much reality, faith first clears the ground of false gods. So early Christians were called atheists by their pious opponents because they joined with philosophers and prophets in the task of criticising an over-fertile religiosity. Space had to be made for the mystery of the one true and living God.

The trouble is that we are ill at ease in our disillusionment. When the 'gods' fail we are quick to manufacture new ones. The political Utopian whose dreams have faded discovers mysteries in the processes of 'market forces' and falls down in obeisance to them. The upwardly mobile who have stopped moving adjust to the worship of golf and domestic comfort. The disillusioned are easy prey to the gods. What I want to insist on at this point is that instead of being hustled into new faiths, yes even into Christian faith, we should learn to stand still and try to understand what our disappointment means. Taking the measure of disillusionment, letting ourselves roll it around the mouth and taste its bitterness, is the way to growth and maturity.

The loss of the secular illusion

Instead of becoming withered up in cynicism there is room for some indignation and anger with the gods which have failed. After all we were offered the kingdoms of this world and their glory if we would only give up the superstition of religion, trust to reason and claim our freedom to seek goals of our own making. To be fair this secular gospel has left us better fed, better housed and more comfortable. Yet it has bred new problems. As we settle down to enjoy its comforts we are bustled out of our armchairs and told that this style of life is a recipe for coronary heart failure. However much we may imagine that reason has been liberated from super-stition, the impression of our world is not of better order and rationality but of chronic disorder and madness. One minute we claim that population growth is out of control and there are too many mouths to feed and the next we are heaping up mountains of butter and cheese and paying farmers to reduce food production. One minute we perceive that our planet is too small for every man to be for himself, and the next we are plunging back into narrow national self-interest. One minute we pride ourselves that we have laid aside barbarism and become the first to discover the sanctity of human life, the next we are busy stockpiling enough nuclear weapons to destroy this planet several times over or acquiescing in the slaughter of countless unborn children. Such an outburst may be simplistic but the fact has to be faced that the secular promise of a more rationally ordered and humane world has not come near to fulfilment. Instead of being bullied into the sort of uncritical reverence for secularism which we would never tolerate in any religion, ordinary people need to express such anger and indignation.

Of course there are secularists equally critical of the direction in which the world is going but within their faith lies a fundamental difficulty. Where are the common standards which enable such criticism to be coherent, reasonable and effective? By what measure can achievement and failure be assessed? After we have been told to grow up, become autonomous, shake off the tutelage of divine laws and imposed standards and make up our own values, what then happens when Jones makes his goal the unremitting pursuit of pecuniary gain and Smith the sexual exploitation of children? If the sense of obligation becomes thus radically privatised, a matter of individual autonomous decision, and 'ought' reduced to 'what I like', then there is no basis for a common judgement on the success or failure of the human enterprise. In a moral free-for-all where every man decides for himself what shall be accounted good or bad there is no room for common values or agreed judgements, and therefore little point in engaging in moral discussion. As Alisdair Macintyre has shown, such discussion becomes a slanging match or a parade of personal options:

The most striking feature of contemporary moral utterance

is that so much of it is used to express disagreements and the most startling feature of the debates in which these disagreements are expressed is their interminable character. I do not mean by this just that such debates go on and on and on but also that they apparently can find no terminus. There seems to be no rational way of securing moral agreement in our culture. (*After Virtue*, p. 6)

Secularism, by insisting that there is no other meaning, purpose or direction save what autonomous individuals fashion, has locked us in on ourselves and deprived us of any commonly agreed way of measuring success or failure.

Making sense of the heights and depths

Faith claims there is a way out of this situation. It points to meaning, purpose and value, which are not of our fashioning and are more than mere ideals. These are rock-hard realities to which, as to all reality, I must submit. But to discover this possibility of making sense of the world and finding a good-ness which is more than my personal option I have to pass through the very door which secularism forbids. I become a rebel, defying not simply the ideals and expectations which it has set before us but its very understanding of what is taken to be real. I am a subversive undermining those 'twin pillars' between which the secular house has been constructed. To us this house has become stuffy and claustrophobic, unable to contain the full dimensions of human experience, the heights of joy and depths of tragedy which we know to be part of reality. Of course there is plenty of greyness in between, but truth will not let us shut out those extraordinary heights of friendship, love and overwhelming beauty we have experi-enced, nor those terrible depths of bereavement or horror of human wickedness. Any claim to speak the truth about human existence must be able to take the measure of light and darkness as much as of greyness. One reason why the Bible is a richly human book is that it is able to do just that. In the rather pedestrian commonsense of the Wisdom literature and in those sober lists of domestic and civic duties in the New Testament, the greyness of much of everyday

29

life is embraced. In its strange overheated 'apocalyptic', this ordinariness is seen afresh in its glory and ghastliness as if illuminated by sudden lightning: the struggling community of faith becomes 'the bride adorned for her husband' while the persecuting state becomes the hideous 'Beast'. To be truly human is thus to be woken up to see things 'in their true colours', to be alert to what is breathtakingly wonderful and to take the measure of the dark cellar in which lurk all manner of monsters. We must be able to say of the terrorist's killing of an innocent hostage: 'That is wicked; that is something which no cause, however good, can justify.' We must be able to say of some piece of music: 'That is beautiful, with a beauty that is not simply a noise which millions of monkeys equipped with violins would one day produce by chance.' We must be able to say of Mother Theresa spending her time on dying beggars: 'That is good with a goodness which cannot be blunted by any consideration of how very few days or hours of additional life such action has won.' As human beings we have a right to shed tears over wickedness, to wonder and rejoice over beauty and goodness.

Faith as daring to ask questions

But all this is to push our heads through the secular ceiling and talk about goodness, truth and beauty which are more than human artifacts. We find ourselves asking: 'Does this human enterprise with its glory and horror make sense? Is there any meaning to it other than what my mind constructs?' The secularist nanny is always to hand to forbid such childish questions. But Nanny does not know best; she is wrong. To ask questions is human. When she says, 'Those who ask don't get', we reply, 'Only those who ask get.' The endless questions of children may weary adult ears, but what are they but the beginnings of intellectual enquiry? This is the only way we find out anything. Great thinkers are like children, they decline to obey Nanny's exasperated order to be quiet. No dogma, no established findings, no orthodoxies will stop them asking the uncomfortable cheeky question.

Fr Macabe writes:

30

To assert that God exists is to claim the right and need to carry on an activity, to be engaged in research, and I think that this throws light on what we are doing if we try to prove the existence of God. To prove the existence of God is to prove that some questions still need asking, that the world poses these questions for us. (*God Matters*, p. 2)

So faith, instead of handing out pre-packaged answers, is concerned fundamentally to stir up a deep dissatisfaction with answers, to go on insisting that every answer poses further questions:

Proofs for the existence of God point to anomalies in a world picture which excludes the God question. It is, it seems to me, quite anomalous to hold that while it is legitimate and valid to ask 'How come?' about any particular thing or event in the world, it is illegitimate and invalid to ask it about the whole world. To say that we aren't allowed to ask it merely because we can't answer it seems to me to be begging the question. The question is: is there an unanswered question about the existence of the world? Can we be puzzled by the existence of the world instead of nothing? I can be and am; and this is to be puzzled about God. (ibid. p. 3)

Seen like this, faith is in business to stir up questions and to insist that every answer poses yet another question. Beyond every link in the causal chain there is another link, and another and another. To be a truth-seeking human is to recognise this; to be a believer is to recognise that there is no stopping place save in that 'than which no greater can be conceived'. Human rationality does not rest content with life as a nonsensical rag-bag of experiences; it is always reaching forward to make sense of the material spread out before it. Even when we peer through telescopes into the vastness of the universe we continue to make this act of faith that there is sense and coherence to be found. Overwhelmed by unimaginable distances, cut down to less than midget size, we still hold our heads high believing that in them the sense of a universe can be contained. And when spacecraft follows where our minds have pioneered and calculations have been made, we find that this mental imperialism has been justified. Whatever quarrels scientists and believers may have had, it seems the case that they are united in their commitment to unceasing questioning and in their confidence that sense is to be found.

I sadly admit that such radical questioning has not always seemed the hallmark of faith. For Iris Murdoch's Stuart, 'God had always seemed . . . something hard and limited and small, identified as an idol.' Religion seems too often to have caught God in a net fashioned not only of sticks and stones but also of intolerably confident verbosity. Dogmas seem to classify, tabulate and reduce 'that which none greater can be conceived' to an item in a card index. To all this the household of faith must plead 'guilty', and yet within it there has remained alive that Old Testament horror of all human attempts to grasp, whether in physical objects or written words, the irreducible mystery we call God. This mystery must always be beyond our grasp, the massive mountain to which the closer we get the less we can see, the mystery hidden in the clouds of darkness, or blazingly and dangerously bright as the sun.

Great Christian thinkers for all their hammering away at words have seen this:

> I was running to lay hold on God and thus I went up into the Mount, and drew aside the curtain of the Cloud, and entered away from matter and material things, and as far as I could I withdrew within myself. And then when I looked up, I scarce saw the back parts of God; although I was sheltered by the Rock, the Word that was made flesh for us. (St Gregory Nazianzen, *Second Thelogical Oration*, 3)

St Augustine wrote a long book on God as Holy Trinity and used both rational argument and picture language, yet all seems to point away into silence: 'I venture to acknowledge openly that I have said nothing worthy of the ineffability of the highest Trinity, among all these many things that I have already said, but confess rather that its sublime knowledge has been too great for me, and that I am unable to reach to it' (*On the Trinity*, Bk 15.50). Who was a more prolific spinner of words than Thomas Aquinas, more meticulous in his striving for fairness in argument, more committed to sweet reasonableness? But he too confesses: 'All affirmations we can make about God are not such as our minds may rest in them, nor of such sort that we may suppose he does not transcend them' (*De. Div. Nominibus*, 1.ii). The truth made known to us in scripture is 'as a little drop descending upon us ... one cannot in the state of this life behold the thunder of the greatness' (*Summa Contra Gentiles*, Bk 4.10). Christian theology for all its bulk is seen by its finest practitioners to be writing itself into silence.

So theological libraries with their weight of presumptuous knowledge do not encapsulate the Christian thing. They are but a part of this complex package, along with the poetry and music which point to hidden depths, and the architectural works which invite the eye to peer into the darkness beyond. Indeed its central activity of worship, the *opus Dei*, is not the hammering of words but the looking away towards mystery. In this we do not seek to extract inspiration or brace ourselves to do good but are simply glad that the mystery, which eludes our grasp, is most real. Worship does not have to justify itself by its usefulness, it is the work of art which instead of grinding out some laboured message is justified simply because it is there, beautiful, good and true. This is given its clearest and most radical expression in the religious life of enclosed contemplative monks and nuns. They give up their lives for the one thing necessary, having no *raison d'être* save the mystery of God, a sign of folly justified only by the reality of the one on whom they have staked their existence. The religious vocation is the interrogation mark of faith lived out in flesh and blood. Monks and nuns have either wasted their lives for an illusion or indeed discovered the jewel of great price.

The ever deeper mystery

Only when the talking, writing, rational activity of Christians is thus balanced by other activities are we rescued from that aggressive, buttoned-up religion which is described with such merciless accuracy by Patrick White in his novel, *Riders in the*

Chariot. Mrs Jolley is quizzing the eccentric Miss Hare about her faith:

'Are you a Christian?'

'Ah,' sighed Miss Hare, 'it would not be for me to say, even if I understood what that means.'

'I am,' said Mrs Jolley. 'I attended the C of E ever since I was a kiddy.'

And would batter somebody to prove it.

'I mean,' persisted the housekeeper, 'didn't anybody bother with your religious education?'

Miss Hare was too embarrassed to answer.

'So as you believe. You do believe in something don't you?'

Miss Hare hesitated. Then she said very slowly:

'I believe. I cannot tell you what I believe in, any more than what I am. It is too much. I have no proper gift. Of words, I mean. Oh yes I believe! I believe in what I see and in what I cannot see. I believe in a thunderstorm, and wet grass, and patches of light and stillness. There is such a variety of good. On earth. And everywhere.'

'But what is over it?' Mrs Jolley had to burst out.

'That!' Miss Hare cried. 'That! I would rather you did not ask me about such things.'

She had got up, and was swaying and trembling, so that Mrs Jolley became afraid. (p. 58)

Here the sense of authentic faith is glimpsed, not in the brittle aggressiveness of Mrs Jolley's formal religion but in Miss Hare's stumbling failure to find words, in her awed swaying and trembling.

Yet if we shrink from being battered by Mrs Jolley's confidence, we may equally be maddened by Miss Hare's mistiness. Believers cannot give a straight answer to the question, 'Who or what is God?' But how could they? Yes they insist that God is objective in the sense of being most truly real, but not in the sense that he, she or it is one object among many. What is a leopard, we ask? And the reply is, 'an animal', for leopards, like pigs and dogs, have some category or group into which they can be placed. It is not so with God. You cannot add God and man together and make two;

you cannot add together a plum pudding and a geometrical theorem: 'Two what?' we ask. There is no answer. God is mystery, ultimate and irreducible mystery.

But this mystery is not a puzzle to be unravelled, like the mystery in the detective novel which is there only to be dispelled the further we advance in unravelling the clues. Indeed when Christianity claims that, after walking through the mists of faith in this life, we shall at last see God as he is, this does not mean the ultimate dispersal of mystery. It is as if we have been standing on the shore looking out to sea but now the waters are encased in mist. Slowly the mist clears, the sun shines out and we can see, but this seeing means being able to see the horizon which ever recedes from us.

The mystery of persons

Of course we are impatient with such talk about 'mystery', it seems to us nothing more than what E. M. Forster called 'a high-sounding term for a muddle' (*Passage to India*, p. 68). Yet if we can resist such instant dismissiveness and ponder on our experience of other people, we may obtain some clue to what believers are struggling to say. A lot of faces just pass us by – the girl at the supermarket cash desk, the bus driver, those who swirl around us in the crowded street. All these are in a way just 'objects' moving past us, unremarkable and unmysterious. I rarely have time to stop and recall that each one is as much an individual as myself. Yet there are times when I suddenly become conscious that those jostling around me on the pavement are not in fact just a crowd, but a number of unique persons with a particular history and background which is unknown to me. I have looked out of a train window and seen people moving around in lighted houses, and wondered what human dramas were being played out there. Sometimes strangers move in from the circumference of our lives and as they come nearer we become more aware of their mysterious nature. The milkman who calls daily and the man with whom I have taken to passing the time of day become real people, and the strange thing is that as they come nearer they become more not less fascinating and mysterious. I want to know more about them – how their holidays went, whether the child who was ill is now better, whether they got to that football match last Saturday. This growth of mystery through familiarity is experienced in those who are closest to us. The woman I love, the children I have, these make up my inner circle and yet are the most mysterious of all. I can truly say of them 'they are beyond me!'

In this human experience we are given a clue to the mystery of God. When asked by opinion pollsters many will say they believe in God, yet if the questioning is more sophisticated it might emerge that the God they say they believe in, like the girl at the cash desk, is on the circumference of their lives. God is there, useful at times but of no abiding interest. He is like the ornament we once bought in Blackpool which rests in honour on the mantelpiece – familiar, treasured but hardly noticed. Such a God neither fascinates nor mystifies. But for the one for whom God is most real, mystery grows with fascination; nearness to God means an ever greater sense of his beyondness.

God's freedom to be himself

The terms 'transcendence' and 'immanence' are often used of God in a mistaken way, the former to denote his distance 'up above the world so high', and the latter to denote his nearness, that 'in him we live and move and have our being'. Put like this there is a conflict between 'transcendence' and 'immanence' and the impression is given that the believer has to strike the right balance, the golden mean, not too much transcendence and not too much immanence. The result is an unsatisfactory compromise, the God of the half-way house, neither near enough to be of interest nor far away enough to be quite safe. But as our experience of human relationships shows, we have got this all wrong. If we ask the question 'Where is God?' the answer must wholeheartedly be that of immanence, God is near, closer to you than you are to yourself. We indeed live by the very breath of God. The answer of 'transcendence' is given to the very different question, 'Who or what is God?' To that question the answer must be that if God is in everything, everything does not add up to God.

The stone is in the box but the box is not the stone. They are different. So God and the world are different. Transcendence then is to do with God's freedom to be himself: 'I am God and there is no other . . . I will be what I will be.' And is this not something of what we have been wanting to say about people? We want to be close to them but we do not want them to be extensions of ourselves, rather we want them to be themselves. The closer I am in love the more I treasure the uniqueness of the one I love, rejoicing that the other is other and not myself.

Countering the attempts to restrict God's freedom

Idolatry is using God as an extension of ourselves. It takes many forms. One is that of magic, the attempt to tap divine power for our own ends. This is easy to detect in its crude forms but it can slip subtly into prayer. Jesus encourages us to ask for things, whether for ourselves or for others, and this because God wants us as we are, natural and without the mask of that false piety which represses human longings. Indeed in the Garden of Gethsemane, the Son of God shares our desire to avoid suffering and death and asks that this cup should pass him by. 'Ask and you will receive,' says Jesus, but what he does not say is that we shall necessarily receive what we have asked for. Jesus did not get what he had asked for; the cup did not pass by; he had to endure the torture of crucifixion. What delivers his prayer and ours from the taint of magic, from using God, is its openness to God expressed in the progress from asking to the genuine, though costly, addition, 'nevertheless not my will but yours'. That is not simply hedging bets but the recognition that God is no slot machine, no impersonal power to be tapped; he is 'himself' with, as we should say, 'a will of his own'. 'Thy will be done' is the acceptance that there is something more to the matter than my saying what I want. It is not the cry of resignation after we have failed to persuade God to our way of thinking but the perception that God in fact loves us more wisely and far-sightedly than we love ourselves, so that to say 'thy will be done' is to ask for what is unimaginably the best.

This is one practical way in which the believer affirms

God's freedom to be himself. Another way is being content to be silent before God's otherness, which is called contemplation. Praying we use pictures of God, those rich images of the Bible, Father, King, housewife hunting for lost housekeeping money, solid Rock, husband, shepherd, and so on. All this is good, for faith, as we have argued, addresses the imagination. But as we move forward in prayer we see that none of these can contain the mystery, that we have to look through and beyond them to the horizon to which they can only point. This pressing forward through images to rest content in the hiddenness of God is what contemplation is about and it too bears witness to God's freedom to be himself. Again this connects with our human experience. With those we love we talk much, and through words try to share something of ourselves. But a moment comes when chatter is stilled and we are content just to be there in the presence of the beloved. At no other moment do we accept and rejoice more in the unique mystery of the other.

The prayer of the seeker

But all this seems to be racing on too far, bustling us from a sense of the mysteriousness of things to contemplation of the mystery of God. Yet it seems to me that in practice this language of prayer, although it bristles with assumptions the seeker is not ready to accept, often rings bells with him in a way which no plodding apologetic can. He finds himself wanting to pray but wonders whether he can honestly do so.

Clearly there are forms of meditation as appropriate to the atheist and agnostic as to the believer. To carve out an oasis of silence in our noise-filled image-battered existence is humanly a good thing to do, for this is a way of preventing ourselves from being submerged in the onward passage of life, of asserting that we are more than corks bobbing on the sea.

When I was an undergraduate in Oxford I was at a college where 'gentlemen' were still expected to attend chapel every Sunday. An unbelieving friend of mine went to the Provost to register his conscientious objection to this practice and was somewhat abashed to be told that, whether he believed in anything or not, it was no bad thing to have an hour's quiet reflection every week. Although I always doubted the possibility of this against the background of the preacher's monologue and the choir's hearty rendering of the *Te Deum*, one could see the Provost's point. But the seeker wonders whether he can advance beyond such uncommitted reflection to make the address *Dominus et Deus* while under his breath adding the qualification, 'if there be *Deus*'. I am sure he can, for there are times when believers find themselves in a similar situation, oppressed with the sense of God's unreality, feeling as they pray like madmen talking to themselves. So I find words and images of faith going dead, sounding like dry peas rattling in a tin and prayer becoming a hanging on by a thin thread: 'O God if you are real, I want to want to pray. Lord I half believe, help my half-belief.' Of course there are important differences between the seeker and the wobbling believer, yet the elements in this experience which are common to both should show that the divide between seeker and believer is not as clear-cut as we imagine.

The believer remains a seeker and the seeker may have in him more of faith than he recognises. This is not really surprising as both of us, whether we recognise it or not, are being drawn towards the same ultimate mystery. To the seeker we should say: 'Do what with integrity you can. If you wish to pray, then pray and if you are minded to use resources of Christian spirituality, do so. These treasures are not for "members only"; they are there for the taking.'

The mystery that makes good sense

However I do not pretend that this sensitivity to mystery is the same as the Christian belief in God. We have arrived at a form of agnosticism, not I think the lazy agnosticism of those who do not know because they have given up asking, but that genuine agnosticism which is as critical of secular as it is of religious idols. But what sort of face does this irreducible mystery show? Religious people assume too blandly that it must of necessity be benevolent. Perhaps this is because religious people are often also comfortable people, and being comfortable make the mystery in the image and likeness of

39

their comfort. So much seems to depend on where we stand in the world. If life is sweet, if we are surrounded by the love of others, have a nice home, a secure job, sufficient money and live in a pleasant environment, then it is not so difficult to believe in a benevolent deity. But what if our position be moved to the grey inner city, a labour camp, or the tin shacks of refugees? What if we are struggling for survival or have become victims of some unjust oppressive regime, if we are unemployed, homeless and unloved; does not the mystery then take on the countenance of wrath? If we are to be realists and not escapists we dare not close our eyes to the dark side of human experience. Yet even this should not prevent us from seeing the light which can break through in the most dire and depressing conditions. Dark glasses are as inadequate as rose-tinted ones for reading our world. The truth is that there is often more of laughter and love to be seen in the faces of the poor and disadvantaged than in those of commuters heading for the suburbs in the crowded underground train. We dare not trivialise the darkness of suffering but we also dare not miss the light.

But then if life is this mixture of light and darkness, should we not read from it a mystery of endless conflict between good and evil, an ultimate dualism? Something deep within us seems in the end to tip the balance in the direction of optimism. The Baron von Hugel told how his daughter arrived on the scene of a terrible earthquake in Italy: 'There lay before her the wreckage and the ruin, the apparently blind and stupid carnage inflicted upon sentient, homely mortals by sheer physical forces, gas and fire.' And yet amidst all this she saw an ordinary priest going about his work: 'He was carrying two infants, one in each arm, and wherever he moved he brought order and hope and faith into all that confusion and despair. She told me that it made them all feel that somehow, love was at the ultimate bottom of all things' (*Essays and Addresses*, 1st ser., p. 297).

In the darkest hours people often seem gripped by the conviction of the ultimacy of goodness, that this thing so little, poor and crushed is yet stronger than chaos and evil. Such a defiant stubborn instinct can be asserted through a sense of humour. When everything is going wrong people still say,

'You can't help but laugh.' It is also asserted in our sense of rebellion against suffering. Confronted by injustice or natural disaster, we do not react with the acquiescence of the dualist: 'That's life – a mixture of good and evil. That's the way the cookie crumbles'; but we rebel and struggle against it. We are not fatalists. This looks like something more than the brave idealist's challenge to the way things are, a conviction that the hope which springs eternal issues not from dreams but from the rock of what is real. The joy which pops up where it seems to have no right to be, appears as solid as the mountain peak peeping out through the clouds, and so gives to those who struggle against evil a strange blend of courage and serenity.

In Camus's novel *The Plague* a doctor fights against deadly disease. He is a figure of immense courage who works in the certainty that nothing he can do will halt the spread of the plague. It has come mysteriously and it will go equally mysteriously. All he can do is shake his fist at this monstrous reality by alleviating as much suffering as he can. It is a noble picture of secular man carving out his little oasis of value in a meaningless world. A few years ago I met a man who in some ways resembled Camus's doctor. Amidst the carnage and rubble of Beirut he struggled to run an orphanage for children disabled in that terrible war. Again and again the orphanage was damaged by shelling. More and more crippled children needed his care. The work seemed a brave but hopeless gesture in the face of reality. Yet to the courage which he shared with Camus's doctor he added something else, a sense of optimism, a conviction that these green shoots of compassion in a cruel desert place counted for more than all the monstrous burden of evil. For him, although life was a muddle as well as a mystery, the mystery was stronger than the muddle and made sense, good sense.

4

The Holy and the Homely

I was brought up in the West country and grew to love the warm gentle, enfolding nature of its countryside. When we moved to the north-east we discovered on the Durham moors a different type of beauty, which overawed and cut us down to size. I suppose since then I have wanted to have the best of both worlds, to be embraced by softness and overwhelmed by wildness. As human beings we seem to need both the security of feeling at home and the excitement of exploration into wild places. G. K. Chesterton fancied writing 'a romance about an English yachtsman who slightly miscalculated his course and discovered England under the impression that it was a new island in the South Seas'. Granted he may have felt rather a fool landing 'to plant the British flag on that barbaric temple which turned out to be the pavilion at Brighton' yet, Chesterton insisted, 'his mistake was really a most enviable mistake. What could be more delightful than to have in the same few minutes all the fascinating terrors of going abroad combined with all the humane security of coming home again?' (*Orthodoxy*, pp. 12–13.) The traveller had stumbled upon the answer to one of life's great questions: 'How can we contrive to be at once astonished at the world and yet at home in it?' (ibid. p. 14).

The draw of Christmas

It is a feeling for this which continues to draw people to the Christian celebration of Christmas, to midnight mass and carol services. Here is that blend of wonder and welcome we are after, a reliving of a story in which the familiar is surrounded by awe-inspiring mystery. A young couple looking

42

for lodgings in a crowded town, cold shepherds at their work on a hillside, the birth of a baby; these are the features of a truly homely story. But there is more to it than that. The celebration fails to do its job if it is stripped of mystery, if painfully relevant songs and cribs bearing a too obvious social message edge out the supernatural. Even if mystery degenerates into magic and angels become conformed to pantomime fairies, this at least indicates that we want something more than the plain and ordinary. Just as the pantomime is not complete without its 'transformation' scene with the wretched unwanted serving girl raised from rags to riches, so in the Christmas celebration there has to be transformation, although here it is the reverse movement from glory to rags, the divine Son for our sake becoming poor. In both cases the drama only works when the contrasts are embraced, when the ordinary is made glorious and the glorious is embedded in the ordinary. Carols proclaiming overwhelming greatness focused in littleness echo an ancient Christian theme. St Hilary celebrates the paradoxical conjunction in this way:

> He who upholds the universe, with whom and through whom are all things, was brought forth by common childbirth; He at whose voice archangels and angels tremble and heaven and earth and all the elements of this world are melted, was heard in childish wailing. The invisible and incomprehensible whom sight and feeling and touch cannot gauge, was wrapped in a cradle. (*De Trinitate*, Bk 2.25)

This Christmas spirit spills over into feasting and festivity, which, far from being a sign of modern degeneracy, has always adorned the Christian celebration. The so-called ages of faith were as materialist and a good bit more boisterous than we are. However drained of faith, the blend of mystery and homeliness continues to be articulated. Decorations turn the familiar home for a while into a palace; the ordinary family meal becomes a veritable feast; the daily exchange of giving and receiving turns into a showering of gifts. For a moment life is seen in a new way, not flat and dull but the carrier of glory. Our exploration may only lead us back to

Brighton beach but we have had the opportunity of discovering it anew:

> We shall not cease from exploration
> And the end of all our exploring
> Will be to arrive where we started
> And know the place for the first time.
>   (T. S. Eliot, *Little Gidding*)

This theme runs through the whole Christian thing. Medieval mystery plays continue to warm modern audiences with their blend of awe and humanity. The old story is embellished with non-biblical detail – the comic Noah and his nagging wife, Herod a figure of folly. This touch of the music hall is genuinely biblical in spirit for the Bible presents life thus, in the raw, vulgar, sinful and yet penetrated with the glory of God's action.

The coming near of the holy

Peter Brook provides a telling illustration of this coming near of the 'holy':

In Haitian voodoo all you need to begin a ceremony is a pole and people. You begin to beat the drums and far away in Africa the gods hear you call. They decide to come to you and, as voodoo is a very practical religion, it takes into account the time that a god needs to cross the Atlantic. So you go on beating your drum, chanting and drinking rum. In this way, you prepare yourself. Then five or six hours pass and the gods fly in – they circle above your heads, but it is not worth looking up as naturally they are invisible. This is where the pole becomes so vital. Without the pole nothing can link the visible and invisible worlds. The pole, like the cross, is the junction. Through the wood, earthed, the spirits slide, and now they are ready for the second step in their metamorphosis. Now they need a human vehicle and they choose one of the participants. A kick, a moan or two, a short paroxysm on the ground and a man is possessed. He gets to his feet, no longer himself, but filled with the god. The god now has form. He is someone who can joke, get drunk, listen to everyone's complaints. The first thing that the priest, the Hougman, does when the god arrives is to shake him by the hand and ask him about his trip. He's a god all right, but he is no longer unreal; he is there, on our level, attainable. The ordinary man or woman can now talk to him, pump his hand, argue, curse him, go to bed with him – and so nightly, the Haitian is in contact with the great powers and mysteries that rule his day. (*The Empty Space*, p. 71)

That description is pregnant with ideas and images familiar to the Christian. St John presents Jesus as being himself the 'ladder' which, like the voodoo pole, connects heaven and earth (John 1:51). The Man of Nazareth is the 'image of the invisible God', the God with form and shape, no longer unreal but 'on our level, attainable'. 'He himself has suffered and been tempted . . . [and] is not ashamed to call us his brethren' (Heb. 2:18,11.)

The holy and the homely in liturgy

To continually bring alive this sense of the homeliness of the holy, there is the Christian ritual which needs only the table, bread and wine and the people gathered. In this, mystery must be neither defused nor distanced. If the liturgy is just plain and matey, a way of stimulating pious emotion or a didactic piece of religious education, it fails to articulate what we are after. Nothing overwhelming seems to come to us. But if on the other hand it is too crowded with symbols of mystery, the holy is made remote and inaccessible. Liturgy communicates when what we cannot grasp or pull to earth is seen to come to earth as gift and so source of further wonderment. Awe is not drained away but rather intensified by the very gratuitousness of the holy being placed into our hands. Grumbles about modern liturgy often contain a genuine and necessary protest against the diluting of the holy. Although blame focuses on flat banal language which is said to lack the depth and evocative powers of ancient 'special' languages, I am convinced that the problem is more one of performance or production. This is not just a matter of conflict between simplicity and elaboration. A very plain liturgy in which the words keep moving into silence can point firmly to the holy, while one overburdened with ritual detail can squeeze out the holy. The production 'works' where the climax of Holy Communion controls the whole celebration; where throughout it is made clear that we are being offered the staggering intimacy of a share in the holy which by coming near never ceases to be holy.

Depart from me Lord! – two ways of distancing the holy

If mystery fascinates and draws, it can also repel. We may want to thrust it away, crying, 'Depart from me Lord,' sensing that the holy one is intrusive and threatening. When the psalmist cries: 'O Lord you have searched me out and known me', while we grasp something of the wonder and joy of this we often miss the note of panic and fear in his prayer: 'Behind and before you besiege me . . . O where can I go from your spirit and where can I flee from your face?' (Ps. 139). Here is a man on the run from God, looking everywhere for some shelter from his all-seeing eye. Because the holy can appear interfering and threatening, forms of religion are fashioned to keep him at bay, polite formalities which allow us to doff our hats to a distant 'Almighty' and give him what we consider to be 'his due', while firmly barring him from intervention in business, political or personal matters. Like the servants, God is expected to keep his place. If he is a monarch he is yet a constitutional monarch, surrounded with formal honour, even allowed to make a speech from the throne, but the words of that speech are those we have written and put into his mouth. Such was the sort of religion called for to embellish the Falklands War victory celebrations; God would be wheeled in to grace the occasion but would not be allowed to raise any disturbing questions. It was a sound instinct which led church authorities to decline such practical atheism masked by public deference.

Of course there is a more serious religion of the distancing of God, one which seeks to guard the mystery from contamination with earthiness. While the holy cannot be allowed to descend, we may yet through spirituality ascend to it. Instead of the ladder set up by God himself in the man Jesus of Nazareth, we set up a ladder ourselves which will take us away from flesh and blood. If God is accessible it is only to some divine portion of myself which has to shake itself free of its earthly fetters to ascend where it belongs, as a spark to be reabsorbed in the blazing fire of divinity. For the body is a tomb which imprisons the eternal soul and salvation is the escape of the soul from that tomb. One has to admit that such a religion, for all its nobility, can never be for more than an élite, the very few who have the time, energy and inclination to tred this arduous path out of materiality to such an immaterial mystery. Thus as this tiny band of athletes struggle up the ladder they inevitably move out of reach of their sensual earthbound brothers and sisters. The nearer they get to this God the further they are from the generality of their neighbours. The few get to the top; the many are left behind.

Seeing how unsatisfactory, formal and mediocre much popular religion is, faith of such toughness and purity cannot but be attractive to the sensitive believer. Here God is taken seriously. Here is that single-mindedness which is ready for the sake of the pearl of great price to sell all. Clearly the lumpen body of the half-hearted needs such disinfecting salt. But it can be demonic and destructive. Where the spiritual athlete dares to soar beyond the flesh of Jesus to some superior knowledge higher than the 'simple faith' of the rank and file, he moves away from that faith which sees God not as the heights to which the mystic scrambles, but as the one who descends to sinful and undeserving shepherds on a hillside as pure gift. Where the believer so leaves behind him the ranks of that grubby mixture which is the household of faith and sets up his own church of the 'pure', he has in fact abandoned the one whose delight it is to mingle with taxgatherers and sinners.

Here we must again insist that the perils of spirituality are greater than perils of the flesh. 'The publicans and harlots go into the kingdom of God before you' (Matt. 21:31). By escaping from the lust of the flesh and the greed of possessions you have not escaped the lure of evil. You may scorn the illusion that overwhelming mystery can be caught by sticks

47

and stones. You may have broken through the simple picture language of faith to those austere impressive-sounding abstract descriptions of deity as 'the Eternal, the Impassible, the Infinite'. Standing on the mountain top where you breathe the clear rarefied air of his presence, you may be unconscious that the mystery can be even more firmly imprisoned in your abstractions, more subtly fashioned to the image and likeness of your pure spirituality. Is the mystery now really free – free to be the shepherd of his flock, king of his world, the husband mourning over his faithless wife? But you may have passed even beyond those clean sanitised abstractions into pure silence. Without any words at all you are content simply to experience God. But then may you not quietly slip into an idolatry of your experience, find the mystery encased in the limitations of what you feel about him?

Evil does not recognise any 'no-go' areas. So the authentically holy have always been those most sensitive to the presence of evil in their pilgrimage. Originally the flight into the desert was not seen as escape from the fleshpots of a contaminating civilisation, but a going forward into the place of the demons and therefore an enlisting in the front line of the battle with evil. With such alertness to evil goes a hesitation amounting to downright scepticism about so-called religious experience. St John of the Cross writes of alleged special revelations and visions that they 'may be true and sure and yet we may be deceived by them . . . the best and surest course is to train souls in prudence so that they flee from these supernatural things, by accustoming them to purity of spirit in dark faith' (*Ascent of Mount Carmel*, Bk 2. XIX).

Holiness and homeliness – the joining together of what has been put asunder

The Christian thing stands for the binding together of what is so often torn apart; that search for the God near at hand which can slip into superstition and that search for the God beyond which can become an élitist denial of love. The world into which Christianity came was torn by these conflicting religious movements. There was the faith of the philosophers, increasingly critical of the many gods of popular religion, and in search of an ever purer grasp of mystery. To such the austere monotheism of Judaism, with its refusal even to write the divine name, appealed. Yet competing with this was the longing of the people that the holy should be near, familiar and relevant; for a God you could feel at ease with. Coming into a culture in which the holiness and homeliness of the deity seemed in conflict, the gospel was proclaimed as the eternal word made flesh, the divine mystery made accessible to sensual humans. This was affirmed, not just in words but also through the use of finite things; the holy made visible and near through bread, wine, water and oil; witnessed to through carved wood and stone, the use of paint and the use of music. Christianity boldly wove a network of sensible signs through which the holy could go on coming near to fleshly humans as the holy had come near in the Man of Nazareth.

God's freedom to have his say

This is no imprisonment of the holy but the recognition of the freedom of God to get his own word in. Our primary task is not to speculate but to allow him to have his say. If transcendence means God's freedom to be himself then it is at least possible that he will wish to communicate with us. Transcendence cannot be used to lock God into compulsory silence. Christianity dares to affirm that God does thus choose to communicate with human beings. He does this not simply to convey esoteric information or give moral instruction but supremely to communicate himself. His communication is thus seen as truly personal, an invitation into dialogue and friendship. Jack may communicate with me by giving information – that there is a particularly good cheap offer of dog food at the local supermarket – or by giving instructions telling me to stop putting my garden rubbish over the fence – or simply to draw me into friendship. It may begin with exchanging views on cricket or politics over a glass of beer at the local, but we may advance from there and Jack may begin to let his hair down and pour out his troubles. Now he is revealing himself.

As we have already suggested, we are all mysteries to one another and through greater knowledge mystery is not dispelled but intensified. None the less we can communicate; these mysteries can be shared. But for such sharing to take place language of some sort has to be used. We can only make ourselves known through words or signs. Human communication is no purely spiritual thing. We may talk of being kindred 'spirits' but we know that we only discover this through language, which is inescapably physical – the movement of lips, the expressions on a face, and so on. It cannot be otherwise if the infinite God is to communicate with finite beings. If he would express himself, seek to share the mystery of himself with us, he can only do so by coming down to our level and connecting with our human world of discourse. So the Christian tradition speaks of the words and gestures of God. It says that these have been heard and glimpsed in fragmentary and varied ways in that tradition of Israel which is available for us in the Old Testament, and which have come into sharp focus centred on the words and gestures of one man, Jesus of Nazareth. Indeed it is claimed he not only speaks the words of God but is himself the Word made flesh.

God's speech through action

Here we must say something about the alleged actions of God. 'Actions', we say, 'often speak louder than words.' Jack will extend his friendship in amiable conversation in the pub, through that more serious speaking from the heart; but also through neighbourly actions, his handing a cabbage over the garden fence or putting himself out for me in time of crisis. Through such actions I know Jack to be someone to whom I can turn. So believers insist that God extends his friendship not only in words but in action. Indeed both in the tradition of Israel and in the gospels word and action go together. God's word is not a 'mere' word, it is the word which explodes into action:

> As the rain cometh down and the snow from heaven and returneth not thither but watereth the earth and maketh it bring forth and bud, that it may give seed to the sower and bread to the eater; so shall my word be that goeth forth

out of my mouth; it shall not return unto me void, but it shall accomplish that which I please and it shall prosper in the thing whereto I sent it. (Isa. 55:10,11)

Much of the Old Testament is taken up with the bustling activity of human beings, stories of kings ruling, slaves escaping from bondage, battles being fought, men and women making love; but it is the consistent theme of the prophetic writers that, in and amidst all this genuinely human activity, is to be discerned the activity of God through which he makes his mind and purpose known. The same marriage of word and deed is seen in the life of Jesus. The people, Mark tells us, were amazed by the power of his words: 'What thing is this?' they asked, 'What new doctrine is this? For with authority he commandeth even the unclean spirits and they do obey him' (Mark 1:27).

But can God act?

Some theologians, including Maurice Wiles, Regius Professor of Divinity at Oxford (see *God's Action in the World*), wonder whether we can take literally such talk of God's 'action'. In the past this was seen in odd and dramatic events – earthquake, plague and lightning, which seemed inexplicable – but as the gaps in human knowledge have been filled so the God 'explanation' has been in retreat. There seems no place for it. So the astronomer could gaze through his telescope into the starry heights and announce that he no longer had any need of the God hypothesis. The universe has been demystified so that, the argument runs, everything is now, at least in principle, explicable. How, as we peer into the closely interlocking chain of cause and effect, can there be room for God 'doing' things?

This problem in fact is not very different from that of the reality of human freedom. Here too we encounter cause and effect seemingly squeezing out the possibility of free choice. 'Freedom language' – I choose to do this and not that – is in fact an illusion. What are we really but the victims of our environment, our genetic inheritance, our psychological make-up or the economic conditions in which we live? There is enough truth in such determinist pictures to make us question the assertion of Rousseau that 'man is born free but is everywhere in chains'. In fact traditional Christianity has also questioned such a simplistic view and seems nearer to the determinist, at least in insisting that complete freedom is the goal rather than the starting point of the human journey. Man, Paul would say, is born in chains and everywhere awaits the glorious liberty of the children of God (Rom. 8:21).

Yet against the determinist the Christian shares with others the conviction that, if we do not have unlimited freedom, most of us have enough, most of the time, to be accounted responsible for our actions. However difficult it may be, in theory, to relate the truth of this sufficient freedom to the truth that there is an explanation for all that we do, we act on this supposition and order society believing that freedom is not illusory. For instance we generally send criminals to prison and not to psychiatric hospitals. But if we are enmeshed in the tight web of cause and effect and yet know freedom, not in the gaps of this web but through it and despite it, the same can be said to be true of God. If in principle all my actions have a naturalistic explanation and yet I am free, the universe can in principle be totally explained and yet leave room for the free action of God. If I can truly call my action my own, then so too can God.

But Maurice Wiles goes on to point out a familiar problem which confronts us in the reality of evil. If God acts to heal Jones of cancer, why does he not apparently act to heal Smith who suffers in the same way? If he intervenes to save a few slaves from bondage in Egypt why did he not intervene to do the same for their descendents in Nazi Germany? With part of this problem we shall be concerned in a later chapter, but here, if we are to maintain belief in the coming near of the holy, we need to face the apparently random results of that coming near. What is Professor Wiles's remedy? He believes that our problem is eased if we posit, not many, but only one action of God, that of creation. I hasten to say that Professor Wiles does not see this action as a once-for-all event in pre-history but as God's ongoing bringing into being of the world. Through this one continuous creating action God lets his world be itself and run itself, and does not, nanny-like, keep intervening. Although the problem is narrowed down it does not really let God off the hook of ultimate responsibility for such a world where cancer strikes at random or which throws up the atrocities of Auschwitz. By removing the difficulty of God's arbitrary intervention, healing Jones but not Smith, coming to the rescue at the Red Sea but not in Auschwitz, Wiles ends with the not very consoling thought that God intervenes nowhere! That may make things fairer but it is a rather bleak fairness and the problem he has raised is not in fact solved; God is not absolved of responsibility for letting these horrors happen. If Nanny decides that the children are now grown up and responsible enough to be left alone, is it not still her responsibility if one of them, lapsing into more childish ways, gets burnt in the fire? In short I cannot see how reducing the number of God's actions to one really solves what is, of course, an agonising problem.

A tempting way of talking about God's action is to claim that we are dealing with different stories of action, which, because they run parallel, do not intersect. One story is that of natural cause and effect as told by the scientist, sociologist, psychologist or historian. The other is that of the drama of God's redeeming and judging action as told by religion. Both stories are true, but the truth of each will not be grasped if they are muddled up. If you like, the scientific story is plain prose while the God-story is poetry. If as an optician I gaze into your eyes I see one set of things; as a lover I shall see another. The solution looks neat and certainly does away with any conflict between the Genesis stories and scientific explanations of the origin of things, but in the end it runs up against the stubborn, and to my mind irremovable, Christian claim that God has not been content to run parallel with the human story, that the poetry of the divine life has been turned into prose, or to put it another way the prose has taken off into poetry. The Word has been made flesh, the God-story has been lived out in and through a human story.

I suspect that Professor Wiles is captivated by this 'parallel-story' model. He reveals this in his discussion on the relationship between nature and grace. So that, he argues, after making an important decision: 'I may say to the friend who has stood by me and encouraged me, "It's all thanks to you!

53

It's all your doing" ' (*God's Action in the World*, p. 99). Now that, Wiles continues, 'would be misleading if taken literally as a straightforward account of the genesis of my action. . . . It really was my action yet my friend's influence in the decision making could be equally real.' So far I can follow the professor but I am bound to say that I think he is mistaken when he argues that the presence of the friend 'needs no particular identifiable initiative to give it its significance' (ibid. p. 105). My friend's influence cannot be dissolved into some vague overall influence divorced from the particular words he has spoken and the gestures of reassurance he has made. Wiles seems not only too 'spiritual' in talking about God's communication but too 'spiritual' in talking about man's. We do not influence one another in a disembodied way but through the particularities of words and deeds. Of course influence cannot be reduced to a bare list of such actions but it does not exist without them. Maurice Wiles is quite right then to insist that we are held in the continuing friendship of God's ever creative love which can never be narrowed down to his 'mighty actions', but he is surely wrong to imply that we can know this love without those particular actions which communicate that friendship. The actions of God are not occasional incursions of divine power but expressions, for our sake, of his enduring love.

The narrowing of universal love?

Yet we are still left with what has been called 'the scandal of particularity', the apparently intolerable narrowing down of allegedly universal love. In the Christian tradition the words and actions of God seem limited to the context of Judaism and the circle which centres on Jesus of Nazareth. The claims of biblical religion seem exclusive. If God really does wish to communicate with the whole human race, is it not more reasonable to expect him to do so through all the varied religious experience of mankind? This would not only be 'fairer', it would evidently assist the growth of tolerance and human unity. In place of its craggy divisive claims, Christianity could take its place as one glimpse of the overwhelming mountain of mystery.

This 'scandal of particularity' is no longer a remote theoretical issue, for with Muslim mosque and Hindu temple now just round the corner from us, we see that there is no room for religious parochialism. Indeed Christians have to recognise with shame their ignorance of and insensitivity to the spiritual riches of other faiths. I cringe with shame at the memory of a devout follower of the Prophet telling me how the local vicar had told him he was an idolater, a worshipper of sticks and stones. Yet it is neither respect nor sensitivity to try to distil from the glories of particular religions some common amalgam of insights. What is refined by this process never quite matches the vigour of the parent bodies. Syncretism, 'we're all going the same way', seems to produce only a bloodless compromise, a paper religion, a disembodied faith, for which only a small élite can generate enthusiasm; while creative dialogue and a genuine sharing of insight come from those who have dug deep to the roots of their tradition and have acquired the security and sensitivity to be alert to the riches of their partner.

Inclusive particularity

Indeed if we dig into the particularity of the Christian tradition we shall find that its apparent exclusiveness is set within a framework of thought which is ultimately inclusive. It insists that the God who is believed to have communicated himself at particular times and places has also been 'speaking' elsewhere in fragmentary and varied ways. God is at once the God of Abraham, Isaac, Moses and the prophets, and the God who calls Cyrus the outsider 'his anointed' (Isa. 45:1). The true light which comes into the world in Jesus is the light 'which enlightens every man' (John 1:9). If the presence of God is focused in Jesus, as the rays of the sun are focused by the magnifying glass, this does not mean that the rays of this same presence do not shine elsewhere. In him we all 'live and move and have our being' (Acts 17:28). The apostle Paul, far from calling the Athenians' altar to the Unknown God a blind alley, takes it seriously as a pointer to the true mystery of God: 'What therefore you worship as unknown, this I proclaim to you' (Acts 17:23).

Perhaps a way forward to a sensitive and ungrudging recognition of the presence of God outside the Christian thing lies in seeing Christ as the sacrament, the outward and visible sign of the omnipresent God. Within Christianity the sacrament of the Eucharist is believed to focus the presence of the crucified and risen Christ, to be the particular point where, in the breaking of bread, he is made known to us (Luke 24:35). But it is an incomplete and impoverished devotion which implies that this 'real presence' involves a real absence elsewhere. Indeed the New Testament speaks also of Christ's presence 'where two or three are gathered together' and in the needs of 'the least of the brethren' (Matt. 18:20; 25:31ff). As St John Chrysostom says:

> Remember that he who said 'This is my body', and made good his words, also said, 'You saw me hungry and gave me no food', and 'in so far as you did it not to one of these, you did it not to me'. . . Consider that Christ is that tramp who comes in need of a night's lodging. (Homily 50)

Christ's presence is unveiled in the sacramental sign precisely so that we should be alert to him everywhere. We need the particularity of this presence because we move through the world as sleep-walkers, unaware of the Christ who is always coming to us. If we use this 'sacramental clue' we may discover how the particularities of the Christian tradition alert us to the presence of the true and living God in other religious traditions. Seeing Christ as the sacrament of God will make us God-spotters, those who everywhere expect to stumble upon traces of his presence.

Picking our words – the particularity of communication

But this does not defuse the stubborn particularities of Christianity, which will not allow Jesus to occupy one niche in the pantheon, to be just one aspect of the divine mystery. Yet is this 'scandal of particularity', on closer inspection, quite as scandalous as we had imagined? There is surely an inevitable particularity about all human communication. In trying to say something, especially something important, we are careful to pick our words and do not just babble on, for, despite

Humpty Dumpty, words do not mean just what we choose them to mean, they are particular, and successful communication depends on our respecting this particularity. In no experience is this scandal of particularity more painful than in writing a book for no task is more necessary than the choice of words and the paring away of superfluous ones. How sad it is to cross out that engaging turn of phrase which distracts from what I am trying to say. Every act of writing is communication through limitation and concentration. All works of art in fact are involved in this scandal of particularity. Just as there is not an endless list of words to be used by the writer, so too there is not an infinite number of notes on the piano, nor canvases of unlimited size for the painter. The musician and painter, as much as the writer, communicate through concentration; their ideas and visions have to be committed to a particular series of notes or a particular square of canvas. If that is the iron law of human communication, and if the eternal mystery of God would communicate with us who are human, how could this be save through a participation in the same scandal of particularity?

Can earthen vessels carry the mystery?

But the more aware we are of the overwhelming mystery of God, the more problematic it seems that this could be communicated to us by means of our limited language. One assured result of a critical study of biblical literature, and of the growth and development of Christian doctrine, is to highlight the time-conditioned nature of the words, images and ideas used. All this hallowed language has not dropped from heaven; the soil of particular times and places clings to it. How could the apostle Paul be so cocky and self-assured as to claim that when he preached, his human words could be received 'not as the word of men but as what it really is, the word of God'? (1 Thess. 2:13). Surely once you have discovered the all too human history of the language of faith, the cat is out of the bag. What was claimed to be the revelation of God is now seen not as revelation but as the response of various cultures to the transcendental mystery of God.

Is there any room now for communication between the

infinite and the finite? It is possible to argue that the communication lies in personal spiritual experience. Words and signs, instead of carrying the revelation, are used to share this experience, to evoke in others the primary spiritual event in which the divine communicates with the human. We can only really speak of 'revelation' when the penny drops, the ice breaks and the individual personally enters into this experience. Although the words and signs remain in the public domain, revelation itself, the moment of disclosure, is thrust into the closet and privatised. Something of a revolution has taken place in the understanding of revelation. But is such a revolution really necessitated by the discovery of the earthiness of religious language and symbolism? Have we not been driven to this conclusion by an undeclared dogma, that the genuinely human and finite cannot be a carrier of the divine word? But this is the very dogma which Christian belief in incarnation challenges. There is a fundamental conflict between this hidden dogma and the belief that the really human can carry the holy.

Although the form of this problem arising from a critical reading of the Bible and Christian doctrine is new, its essential nature is not. Entering a culture deeply impregnated with the belief that earthiness divided the human from the divine, early Christians had to struggle hard to see how the divine in its full integrity could really be made flesh. It seemed radically inappropriate for the holy to become homely. If the divine was to be let in surely something must be missing in the completeness of Christ's humanity, there must at least be some opening, some gap in the human which the divine could fill. To affirm the fullness of incarnation, as Christians did at the Council of Chalcedon in AD 450, meant a revolution in the whole way of looking at the relation between God and humanity. If this was true we were saying something startling, not only about God but also about the extraordinary potential of humanity. Earthiness, our embodied fleshly condition, was no longer to be seen as a barrier between ourselves and God but destined to be the holy tabernacle, the carrier of glory. If Jesus was a real man and was the presence of the undiluted holy in our midst, then earthiness was able to be a sacrament of the divine. However infected and spoilt by evil our material existence might be, it was stamped with the very image of God which we had seen in Jesus, and so at root not bad, but very good. When Leo the Great celebrated the nativity of Christ he cried: 'O Christian, be aware of your nobility – it is God's own nature that you share!' (Sermon 1, Nativity, 1–3). What is at stake in this revolution in the value placed on earthiness is not only the possibility of divine self-communication but also a rich humanism.

We are no angels – on not going beyond the flesh

Obviously this connects with our insistence that real Christianity is not simply a theory for the mind or a way of pure spirituality, but an earthen vessel, a bundle of flesh and blood activities. All this is not just the wrapping but part of the gift itself. The music hammered out on black and white notes takes us beyond the material piano, but it is those solid ivories which are the means of this musical grace. The picture fashioned from daubs of paint may give an intense aesthetic experience, but it only does so in and through the materiality of that paint. No ivories, no paint, no grace. The flesh of the Christian thing cannot be peeled away to lay bare some inner fruit. The Word made flesh only continues to be accessible through this material network of words and signs.

For those who feel at home with ideas this can be burdensome. They long to kick away the ladder and zoom up to the divine. Indeed they have a point. Just as we are enticed beyond material piano and paint, so we have seen that it is necessary to allow the signs and symbols of faith to move us beyond, towards the mystery. In this way we resist God being captured in containers. But, as we have also shown, this movement has perils of its own. The believer who accepts his humanity and does not pretend to be a disembodied angel learns to move between the two positions, aspiring one minute beyond and the next returning to take his place as one beggar among many, holding out empty hands to receive what is given. If the movement beyond purges idolatry, the return purges élitism. We are put in our place, shown that we are always the beginners, the learners, who depend on the waters of baptism, the food of the Eucharist, the word of God's forgiveness spoken through all too human priests.

Even the most ardent spiritual athlete knows moments of weariness and sheer boredom. There are times when he must stop straining forward to relax and allow God to wash his feet. In this I discover that I am always the recipient, the undeserving whose world is constantly bombarded by divine grace. The way to do this is to fall back on Brother Ass, to accept one's humanity by relaxing into faith's network of signs and pictures, to return again to childlike words of prayer, to receive the sacraments, light a candle, listen to music, look at paintings. Where we thus allow ourselves to be served by the earthen vessels of faith, we not only rediscover the homeliness of the holy, but find ourselves toppled from a lone pedestal and plunged into the community of ordinary Christians. The Baron von Hugel, who was a great teacher of aspiring mystics, with a strong sense of the otherness of God, yet daily used the rosary so that, through the physical action of beads running through the fingers while focusing on simple gospel pictures, he might be rooted both in the givenness of faith and in the ranks of the faithful, for whom this is often the staple means of prayer. This was the practical way in which the baron refused to go beyond Jesus come in the flesh and thus refused to go beyond his brothers and sisters.

5

The Personal Centre

In the end nothing matters more to us than the personal. Sit in a bus, go to the pub, stand in the queue for the supermarket cashdesk, and you will hear people chatting; and note that the substance of their conversation is about people, a series of anecdotes: 'he said . . . she said . . . I said'. While the few may like to share ideas, the majority talk for the sake of telling stories about people. Tabloid newspapers know that the secret of success is to give the personal angle on celebrities – the love life of a pop star or snippets of gossip about the royal family. Pure politics are indigestible unless sugar-coated with the human face of our politicians, who, realising this, try to project themselves as sincere caring men of the people. Instead of being cynical, we should see that this bears witness to a central human priority, which says: 'You may hold the highest office in the land, your head may be buzzing with all manner of fine ideas, you may sing like an angel or have us rolling in the aisles with your comic act, but at the end of the day we want to know what you are like as a person.'

The way to God through what is human

Christianity connects with this personal priority. It is above all about people. The more personal it is the better it works. While the argumentation of St Paul in his letter to the Galatians may leave us cold, the personal stories of the Old Testament and the gospels ring bells. While the discussions of theologians and the political manoeuvres of senior clergymen move us not a whit, an ordinary congregation with its mixture of the good, bad and indifferent can at least be interesting. We can speculate on the secret life of the stately lady who

61

marches so confidently into church with fat prayer book tucked under her arm. The godly may sometimes be offended because television programmes make clergymen seem uniformly ridiculous, but is it not better to be ridiculous than to be cold and dull? Dave Allen has a point when he justifies his mockery of religious figures by claiming that it makes them appear human. Being laughable is very near to being lovable. If we are made to mock the pompous prelate and the hypocritical churchwarden we may find that laughter cracks the silly masks they have put on to hide their humanity, so setting us free to discover and love the reality beneath.

It seems a plain fact that nothing so draws us to faith as the godliness which shines out through what is genuinely human. Those who get through to us are not the cardboard cut-out Christians who, aspiring to sanctity, have bypassed humanity and clank around in their ill-fitting armour of faith, but those whose godliness fits their humanity. Just because in them nothing is strained and laboured, they open to us a window into God. The homeliness of the holy centres on the human. Christianity, as we have said, is a complex package. Its signs and symbols are important, its carefully articulated words are important, but these only acquire their importance by pointing to a personal centre, Jesus surrounded by his friends the saints. In heaven, we are told, there will be no temple, no signs, symbols or apparatus of religion (Rev. 21:22), there will just be people caught up in the glory and beauty of the very love of God. So St Paul proclaims the ultimacy of the personal: 'Love never ends; as for prophecy, it will pass away; as for tongues, they will cease, as for knowledge, it will pass away' (1 Cor. 13:8). One suspects that the conversation of heaven will be unlike that of a university senior common room and more like that in a bus, in that we shall rejoice more in people than in ideas.

Because we are already citizens of heaven, those who sample the firstfruits of that harvest to come, the heavenly priorities have to dominate the present Christian enterprise. The heart of the matter has to be our relationship with God through Jesus Christ and our relationship with one another, a working out of the twofold commandment of the Lord. It is to this strong simple centre that everything else must point.

All the apparatus of Christianity exists, not for its own sake, but to plunge us ever deeper into this love of persons. Often we fail to see the wood for the trees, worship becomes a ceremonious formalism, doctrine a set of dreary formulae and the church itself a creaking and corrupt institution, so that we have to hack through it all to rediscover and lay bare what it is about.

Jesus – the living personal centre

While the letters of St Paul show that the apostle's faith is centred on the person of Jesus, they also show that it is disconcertingly unconcerned with the biographical detail of the life of Jesus. What matters seems less what happened once upon a time than a personal relationship with the Man of Nazareth in the here and now, a relationship of extraordinary intimacy: 'I live yet not I but Christ in me. . . The life I live is the life of the Son of God who loved me and gave himself for me.' Being 'in Christ' or Christ being 'in me' – that is the strange language of the apostle.

Indeed there is a startling contrast between this and the relationship between Christ and his followers during his earthly life. In the gospels Jesus seems isolated and lonely, and baffling to his friends who, though near him physically, find him beyond them; they are with him in the flesh but not in understanding. They often seem part of the faithless unseeing, unhearing generation. Nothing so expresses this sense of distance between master and followers than the picture of Jesus setting off for Jerusalem, the place of his forthcoming passion, with his friends trailing behind amazed and afraid (Mark 10:32). But then there was Saul of Tarsus who never met Jesus in the flesh, claiming to 'have the mind of Christ'! We almost have to shake ourselves to realise that, even before the evangelists set down the detail of what happened in Palestine, Christians like St Paul already lived in the conviction that Jesus was in their midst, not the dead hero but the present brother and Lord.

The claim to such an extraordinary experience is not solely of the past to be read about; it is still being made. To encounter it you do not have to sift ancient documents or engage in archaeological research, but simply open your eyes and ears and find out what contemporary Christians are saying. Rather dull ordinary people with their personal language of 'he said . . . she said . . . I said' add this further dimension of conversation with Jesus as if he were a contemporary: 'Jesus, Son of the living God, have mercy on me a sinner . . . my Lord and my God . . . thanks be to thee my Lord Jesus Christ for all the benefits which thou hast won for me.' Whether it be an evangelical, pouring out her heart to her personal saviour, or a Catholic praying before the blessed sacrament, they are united in expressing this relationship.

The raw material of faith

The language of devotion needs to be taken seriously and not treated as a sort of rhetorical flourish. When a Christian today says, 'Blessed be Jesus Christ true God and true man', he is not merely mouthing a traditional formula nor engaging in a poetical way of registering the enduring significance of Jesus of Nazareth; he means what he says. He may be mistaken or deluded but at least he should be given the credit for knowing what he means. It is important to underline this, for the primary data of what Christianity thinks about Jesus lies not in formal dogmatic statements but in the living prayer of the people. A congregation on Christmas morning singing 'O come let us adore him', or a lone believer kneeling before the crib, provides us with the raw material of faith. It is indeed articulated and stamped with the community's seal of approval in dogma so that simple and instinctive faith is both recognised to be more than the product of an individualist 'do-it-yourself' religion, and becomes able to be defended from corrosive sophistication. Yet no wedge can be driven between such personal faith and this later endorsement. I have heard a theologian argue that the church's dogmatic confession about Jesus is mistaken, yet conceding that the language of devotion can be allowed a latitude which careful statements of theology are not. Devotion, he would claim, can take off from the plain prose of what is literally true into poetry and hyperbole. While it may seem ungracious to

decline such an olive branch, we must insist that the imagination cannot be so divided from reason as to make what is
idolatrous untruth in the study become acceptable in church
on our knees. In practice I doubt whether the language of
worship could survive such a double-think. Could we really
put our hearts into hailing 'the incarnate deity' in the
Christmas hymn if we were told from the pulpit that this was
not literally true?

The articulation of faith in the dogma of the Church

Certainly the language of worship often differs from that of
sober doctrinal statement, but the difference is not one of
seriousness and truth. The definition of the Council of Chalcedon articulates the faith that Jesus is true God and true
man in a way which not only goes beyond the language of
twentieth-century devotion but also that of the New Testament. This articulation is made as a result of a process of
genuine development in the understanding of the community.
Everything was given in the witness of the apostolic
community to the living, dying and rising of Jesus. In him
is the revelation of God. This means that the believer in
the first century receives the same gift as the believer in the
twentieth. Neither has an advantage over the other. Yet the
witness to this revelation is committed to the stream of history
and there encounters difficulties to be overcome and the possibility of new insights. As loyal Jews the early disciples were
committed to belief in the one true and living God and thus
shared the Old Testament horror of anything which might
erode the distinction between infinite and finite: 'I am the
Lord, and there is no other, besides me there is no God' (Isa.
45:5); while 'the fate of the sons of men and the fate of beasts
is the same; as one dies, so dies the other' (Eccles. 3:19). But
now as followers of Jesus these Jews, who had not repudiated
their faith, came to believe that the hope and salvation which
could come from God alone had in fact come through this
Man of Nazareth, the very one of whom people had said: 'Is
not this the carpenter, the son of Mary and brother of James
and Joseph and Judas and Simon, and are not his sisters here
with us?' (Matt. 13:55–56). How could these two assertions

be fitted together? As austere Jewish monotheism would not allow a dilution of the deity, might not a solution be found by arguing that the humanness of Jesus was but an appearance, a disguise? Of course the crucifixion was a great stumbling block to this solution. It had therefore to be presented as a piece of playacting with a tortured human body nailed to the cross while his divine spirit floated impassively above.

To an age which can understand Jesus as the wise and witty human teacher but wonders what it can mean to call him Son of God, this problem of how the truly divine could be present in the truly human is puzzling. Yet it was to counteract the instinctive feeling that the blazing fire of divinity must inevitably burn up the finite, that the New Testament had to insist that the Son of God really did partake of our nature (Heb. 2:14). 'By this you know the Spirit of God: every spirit which confesses that Jesus Christ has come in the flesh is of God' (1 John 4:2). The first task of reflective faith was less to hammer home the presence of the divine in the life of Jesus than to affirm that this presence could be there in the genuinely human.

What it means to be human

Our own age has particular insights into what this affirmation must mean, for it has particular insights into what being human means. We no longer see the complete person as a lone individual who can be divided up as body, mind and soul, but as one bound up with others in the bundle of life and firmly set within a particular historical context. To be human is to be set down in one place and not another, thus to inherit a particular language and ways of thought, able to assert individuality and freedom only through using such shared material. To be human is also to be set down in one age, distanced both from the past and the future, on the one hand feeling the gulf between ourselves and our forefathers and on the other turning towards the future with real hopes and fears. This, we say, is what it is to be human. So orthodoxy must involve accepting these truths and boldly applying them to Jesus. He really was a Palestinian Jew of the first century. The divine could only be lived out in and through this rootedness in space and time.

However when we say, and rightly, that Jesus was 'one of us' we should beware of trying to fit him into the image of a stereotyped 'average' sort of man. Such an image hardly accords with the insight of our age which sees the extraordinary potential of humans. Experience has taught us that it is foolhardy to set limits on what is possible to this creature. Although we are 'of the earth, earthy', influenced and moulded by our inheritance, we are always spurring ourselves to go beyond that inheritance, daring to do what our forefathers deemed 'impossible'. If we understand our roots to be firmly in the earth, the sky yet seems to be the limit and today we set out to achieve what yesterday was unachievable. Real humanity cannot be held within the confines of Mr Average Man. Paradoxically, in our contemporary understanding of what it is to be human the insight into man's frailty and bondage to time is combined with a heady vision of his amazing potential for going beyond these limitations.

But this warning against trying to fit Jesus into a dull and modest image of humanity provides no excuse for nervously drawing back from taking the confession 'true man' too far. Orthodoxy does not allow the fearful option of hastening to add a bit more of 'the divine' if Jesus seems to be becoming a bit too human. It has rejected the way of balance and moderation and insists that the divine does not get a foothold in the life of Jesus by reducing the reality of his manhood. It is through the life of the finite that the infinite is lived, in full-blooded humanity that the fullness of Godhead dwells bodily.

The presence of true God

Yet Jesus is acknowledged to be more than the centre of God's activity, more than the head boy in the school of holy men. He is, in those ringing mysterious words of the Chalcedonian definition, 'of one substance with the Father as to his Godhead . . . begotten of the Father before ages as to his Godhead'. These are not of course the words of the New Testament for this is an articulation of faith made possible

by the passage of time, in which faith has sought understanding and its pondering has come under the pressure of
controversy and conflict. What is here expressed is spelt out
in the 'new' terminology of the Graeco-Roman world and yet
it is firmly grounded in the original testimony of scripture. It
is not the case that there was first 'the simple faith' of those
who followed the godly Rabbi and then the complicated faith
of sophistical theologians beguiled by Greek philosophy. The
New Testament lays before us the resounding Johannine texts
which insist that the Word that 'was God' had become flesh
and dwelt among us so that we have beheld the glory (John
1:1, 13–14); that to see Jesus is to see the Father (John 14:9).
There are the texts of the epistles, where Jesus is said to be
'in the form of God' (Phil. 2:6); the one who is 'the image of
the invisible God' (Col. 1:15); in whom 'the fullness of deity
dwells bodily' (Col. 2:9). Certainly I have plucked out the
most startling and controversial texts but, whatever they
orginally meant, they are hardly good examples of 'simple
faith'.

'Ah, but,' the critics say, 'the rot set in early, the corrupting
maggots of sophistication were all too quickly at work.
Already in the New Testament the ethical teaching of Jesus
is being turned into dogmatic catholicism.' Perhaps it is more
convincing to see these great texts as drawing out what is
present in less explicit material. I find myself brooding over
those 'throw-away' lines in which Jesus seems to be slipped
unobtrusively on to the God side of the man-God divide.
Without fuss or trumpet blasts he is seen as the recipient of
worship or as the bestower of divine blessing. 'At the name
of Jesus, every knee shall bow, in heaven and on earth and
under the earth, and every tongue confess that Jesus Christ
is Lord, to the glory of God the father' (Phil. 2:10,11). The
greeting, 'Grace to you and peace from God the Father and
our Lord Jesus Christ' (Gal. 1:3), seems to have already
become formal and liturgical. In the Revelation of St John
the Divine the worship of Jesus has become explicit: 'Worthy
is the Lamb who was slain, to receive power and wealth and
wisdom and might and honour and glory and blessing' (Rev.
5:12).

The developing insight of the community of faith

In such texts we are given precious peeps into the developing consciousness of the Christian community. Their very formality shows that this was something more than the speculations of élitist thinkers leaping ahead of simple faith. The great articulators like Paul and his successors were trying to put into words what a whole community was feeling towards. It was the body of the faithful, which, like Mary, had received the fullness of God's gift in Christ and now kept these things, pondering them in the heart (Luke 2:19,51). It was a genuinely common faith which sought understanding. Before ever theologians hammered out words adequate and accurate enough to express this experience, rank and file Christians were driven to worship Jesus as God. An outside observer, the Roman governor Pliny, whose main concern with Christians was as a matter of law and order, could not but notice that members of this strange sect practised the characteristic activity of singing hymns to Jesus as to a god. A Roman soldier mocked by his fellows could be depicted kneeling to worship a crucified donkey.

The variety of insights

But if in the New Testament we can discern the seeds of the articulated dogma of the incarnation, and are thus able to trace a genuine line from the apostolic witness, through the deepening experience of those who followed, to the dogma of Chalcedon, it is only honest to admit that there are other understandings of Jesus in the New Testament, which, had they been treated as master themes, might have led to other articulations. The so-called heretics were also able to produce their biblical proof-texts and establish a claim to be the guardians of true faith. Critics thus have a point when they say that 'orthodoxy' simply represents the side which won.

It has to be recognised that the New Testament offers a variety of ways of understanding the significance of Jesus. Indeed our reading is enhanced when we learn to savour the distinctiveness of approach and discover where Paul, John, Mark and Luke differ, as well as where they agree. In making this discovery we cannot evade the element of conflict and will find that the Utopian picture of the early church as all harmony and sweetness is replaced by a more robust abrasive one. We can at last take seriously the conflict between Paul and Peter (Gal. 2:11), recognise that there were others besides us who found 'some of the things' in the Pauline epistles 'hard to understand' (2 Pet. 3:16) and realise that there were genuine differences between the style of faith of the Johannine churches and those shaped by the influence of other leaders.

I find that this vigorous variety witnesses the more impressively to the importance and creativity of what happened in Palestine in the events surrounding Jesus. Here are followers overwhelmed, struggling to find words adequate to describe what it all meant. What they could say had to be drawn from the stock of language and images they had inherited. Nothing else was available. Yet see what happens as they handle this tradition! The old wineskins cannot contain the new wine; they burst. Jesus cannot be fitted into the old categories. The old images – prophet, son of David, Messiah – are taken and applied to him, but though they will point they can never contain. They say so much but there always seems more to be said. They have to be twisted and battered to serve their new use and in the end we see that the images do not control Jesus, he controls them. To advance to saying he is God is not to produce one more image, even a super-image, it is to ascribe to him the ultimate freedom of the infinite. Instead of squeezing the Man of Nazareth into our preconceived notions of God, the mystery of what God is is now defined by the matter of fact reality of what Jesus is.

The victory of the master theme – a justified victory

Some believe that the Church should return to this fertile primitive multiplicity of understandings and reject the imperialism of an orthodoxy which has brought the many images under the heel of that one master theme, the dogma of incarnation. In the development of this unitary understanding, it is asked, have we not lost something of the essential Jewishness of Jesus? While the dogma of incarnation makes Christianity exclusive, a return to this primitive multiplicity might bring us nearer to both synagogue and mosque. A whole-hearted acceptance of the variety of the New Testament theologies and ways of ordering the church might also crack the tough nut of Christian disunity and provide a realistic way of handling our differences. We should then learn to turn from the tyranny of one Church with its insistence on doctrinal master themes and uniform order, to the liberty of a variety of churches with a variety of doctrines and styles of order.

However to speak of multiplicity without qualification is to treat the New Testament as an à la carte menu of doctrines and orders from which we are invited to take our pick. And this is to ignore the real unity which the sifting and gathering of these varied documents into one authoritative volume implies. There are ways of doing justice to their undoubted variety which are compatible with their unity. So Hans Urs von Balthasar has spoken of 'the multiplicity and polyphony of divine truth' and insisted that 'the Truth is symphonic', not the monotony of one blasting instrument but precisely the integrating of many instruments in the one performance: 'The orchestra must be pluralist in order to unfold the wealth of the totality that resounds in the composer's mind' (*Truth is Symphonic: aspects of Christian pluralism*, p. 7). But this very variety requires unity: 'the more an organism becomes differentiated and alive in its individual organs and functions, the more it must possess a more profound internal unity' (*Analogy of Beauty*, p. 229). So instead of being invited to pick and choose from this multiplicity we are invited to hear God's 'composition' through the whole New Testament orchestra or, to change the analogy, to see 'the image of the invisible God' set before us by a complex mosaic. This is clearly a richer experience than that of listening to one instrument in isolation, or of gazing at one tiny fragment of the mosaic.

In fact, far from leaving variety behind to become ever more monochrome, the Christian enterprise, as it moves outwards from its Jewish starting point and encounters other cultures, takes on board ever greater variety. More and more instrumentalists are caught up in the orchestra. This rejection of the 'closed shop' and deliberate option for variety as the spice of life means that the task of unity, holding the show together, is a continuing and ever more demanding one. The bigger the orchestra the more necessary the conductor is. So that 'profound internal unity' of which von Balthasar speaks has to be made flesh, externalised so that the riches of variety are held by tough bonds of unity. The stamping of doctrinal master themes and the shaping of an ordered church life, with bishops as centres of local unity and the Pope as centre of international unity, become the ways in which the body copes with multiplicity without being torn to pieces. Of course this preservation of unity is, in the end, for the sake of the individual believer. Instead of being left to choose from an à la carte menu, to pick what fancy item catches the eye, he is assured 'all things are yours' (1 Cor. 3:21) and offered a whole and balanced faith.

In the exhortation to turn from imperialistic orthodoxy to New Testament pluralism lurks a curious fundamentalism, a belief that what is most primitive must be most pure. This neglects the creativity of that process of development which has already started in the New Testament itself. As we shall see later, if we are historians in search of what probably happened all those years ago, we shall have a quite correct prejudice in favour of the most primitive evidence. But if in addition we are searching for an understanding, articulated in the best and fullest way, of what happened, we shall not necessarily choose what is earliest. It takes time to understand the significance of events. Ideas, said Newman, have to be entrusted to the stage of history:

> whatever be the risk of corruption from intercourse with the world around it, such a risk must be undergone, if it is duly to be understood, and much more if it is to be fully exhibited. It is elicited by trial, and struggles into perfection. Nor does it escape the collision of opinions even in its earlier years; nor does it remain truer to itself, and more one and the same, though protected from vicissitude and change. It is indeed sometimes said that the stream is clearest near the spring. Whatever use may be fairly made of this image, it does not apply to the history of a philosophy or sect, which, on the contrary is more equable, and purer,

and stronger, when its bed has become deep and broad and full. (*Development of Doctrine*, p. 100)

What has happened is that the community, which continues to reel under the impact of Jesus of Nazareth, has pursued one line of understanding of him which, opening up from the New Testament, leads to Chalcedon. Orthodoxy in its conflict with alternative understandings is the winning side but is able to produce reasons why its victory is justified. It claims that the choice of this path, and this path only, most adequately reflects its own living experience of Jesus. Sense is made of those prayers which believers address to him and of their communal worship at the Eucharist. Orthodoxy can claim too that the choice of this incarnational master theme, far from narrowing the wide range of New Testament options, in fact includes them and is alone able to embrace and preserve them all. As Cardinal Ratzinger has written:

> While . . . the Church has concentrated in this one word (Son) the structures of a tradition which is so diverse, giving at the same time a final simplification to the fundamental Christian definition, it should not for all that be considered as a simplification in the simplist, reductionist sense; in the term 'son' is to be found that simplicity which is at the same time profundity and amplitude. 'Son' as a fundamental profession of faith, signifies that in this term is given the key interpretation which makes all the rest accessible and understandable. (*Journey towards Easter*, p. 79)

In fact, contained by this simplification and concentration, the many images are secured, not now as a set of alternative options but as necessary parts of the mosaic which confronts us with 'the image of the invisible God' or as members of the orchestra which together play the divine composition.

Reading the gospels

It is to gaze on this mosaic or to listen to this symphony that the Christian reads the gospel story. Just as for the apostle Paul a relationship with the living Christ is central, so it is for the evangelists. The gospels are not detached records but attempts to see what happened in Palestine in the perspective and with the concerns of present experience. Although Luke aims to produce an orderly account of the things which have been accomplished among us (Luke 1:1) he, as much as the writer of the fourth gospel, writes, 'that you may believe that Jesus is the Christ, the Son of God, and that believing you may have life in his name' (John 20:31). The gospels are thus more like party political manifestos than scholarly biographies. They are frankly intended to recruit us for the Christian cause and so show remarkable freedom in arranging the stories of the sayings and doings of Jesus to address contemporary cares and concerns. This fact, which some find disconcerting, puts the Bible reader who seeks some word from God addressed to his own condition close to the evangelists' first readers. They, like us, wanted more than an account of what happened 'once upon a time'. They strained their ears for some echo of the words of that living Christ who is the same yesterday, today and for ever.

It is wrong to believe that such listening for the word of God involves closing ears to the work of modern biblical scholarship. Only if we are haunted by the mistaken belief that what is human and finite is unable to carry the divine shall we find real difficulties. Our faithful reading of scripture is indeed enhanced by an awareness of the different types of material used to fashion the portrait of Jesus and by the recognition that the evangelists communicate not just bare fact but also the meaning of fact.

I once heard an old-fashioned fundamentalist conducting a meditation on the nativity of our Lord. It was plain Christmas card stuff – shepherds, manger, magi and star – all just part of the background. Afterwards a more critical reader reflected on what had been said. If you took the star as just one historical fact, he mused, there was not really much more that could be said about it. But if you started asking the disturbing question 'Was it really there?' then you might be on to something important, for if it was not there, you had to ask why the evangelist had put it there! What was he trying to say by the inclusion of this apparently innocent bit of scenery? Often it is not the uncritical acceptance but the critical questioning which will open up the riches of scripture. For another example, St Matthew says that when Jesus died on the cross 'the curtain of the Temple was torn in two from top to bottom' (Matt. 27:51). If that is just a piece of supernatural fireworks it is impressive, but hardly more. It is only when you look closely at the alleged event and ask what Matthew, in the language and imagery of his day, was trying to say by its inclusion, that you are alerted to the great truth that, through the death of Jesus, the barrier between God and man is broken down. While a marvel once upon a time is interesting but cannot affect me much, I too can now know the greater marvel, that the iron curtain between myself and God has been broken down by the saving cross.

A recognition that the gospel mosaic contains symbol communicating meaning as well as plain fact helps us to read the gospels as they were intended to be read and so enhances our ability to hear the voice of the living Christ addressing our situation. This does not mean that the evangelists had no concern for what actually happened. They shared the conviction expressed in 2 Peter: 'We did not follow cleverly devised myths' (2 Pet. 1:16). The Christ they saw as their living contemporary was no mythological figure fashioned by the intense religious experience of the community. He who was of today was the same Christ as of yesterday.

The Christ of faith and the Jesus of history – are they the same?

The reason we cannot tolerate two sorts of Bible reading, the one pious and naive, the other hard-headed and critical, is that imagination and mind must walk hand in hand. The one who stands on the river's edge complains that the former reading presupposes that the Christ of the believer and the Jesus of history are one and the same, that the gospel mosaic accurately portrays the Man of Nazareth. But this is precisely the issue in question, he claims, that which must be tested. Could it not be that the beauty of the mosaic inhibits us from asking: 'But is it true? Is this what Jesus was really like?' The enquirer's concern is shared by the committed believer for if the Word is indeed made flesh the gospel must, at crucial points, be open to historical inspection. When the nervously orthodox fear such critical probing they in fact connive in the dividing of the 'Christ of faith' from the 'Jesus of history' and so slide unknowingly into what has been called 'modernism'. Their very anxiety for orthodoxy betrays orthodoxy, which requires that rich images and deep understandings be grounded in what actually happened. It must be possible to peer behind the gospel stories to glimpse the Jesus of history. It must be possible to unearth enough material whereby we can judge whether the portrait painted by the believing community is accurate.

Historical investigation – its necessity and limitations

As I have said earlier, this is a point where we can feel daunted or blinded by science, tempted to hand the job over to some group of experts. It is necessary to keep our heads and get this critical probing task into perspective.

Genuine historians are modest people, well aware of the limitations of their craft – and by no means happy to play an authoritarian role – they encourage us to look for ourselves. 'See what we do,' they would say, 'it is in truth not very mysterious. We let down our net into the total sea of fact but are the first to admit that we can catch very little. The mesh of our net has to be wide and through it inevitably will slip many things which have actually happened but have never been recorded. During this day I shall say and do many things which, because they are rather insignificant, will never be accounted "historical events". Yet they have happened every bit as much as the Battle of Waterloo happened. What is judged worthy of being accounted "history" has to follow a process of selection, the sifting of the significant from the trivial. Without this our books would be even more intolerably long than they already are! However we have to admit that what is taken to be "significant" changes from time to time. In recent years a lot of what was once treated as trivial has acquired a new importance. So you will find us burrowing in wills, diaries, recipes and medical prescriptions, for these show us how people lived once upon a time. In fact we have become far less élitist in our concerns, paying attention now as much to the man in the Clapham omnibus as to kings and statesmen. If you were to keep a diary a time might come when the apparently trivial events of your days would be elevated to the status of significant history. The thing which you must keep bearing in mind is that there is an ambiguity about the word "history". It can in common parlance mean everything that has really happened or it can more narrowly mean that little bit of everything of which traces remain and we fallible scholars hold to be of importance. In one way history is the total sea of fact and in another only the fish caught in the historian's net.'

With some such words the modest historian encourages us to take up our task. At once we can see the limitations of any search for the Jesus of history. In terms of the 'great events' of the first century AD, what happened in Palestine was pretty minnow-like and thus slipped through the net of most contemporary observers. The very few who believed that what happened was of significance had a vested interest in this belief. Yet that will not deter the secular historian. 'Good heavens,' he says, 'we are always dealing with material like that. Show me any evidence which is not slanted by vested interest!'

Historians are not only aware of the rough and ready nature of their nets but are used to coping with biased or meagre evidence. See what happens when they come across bizarre or allegedly miraculous happenings. Of such recorded marvels there is an abundance. But the historian keeps his head; he is not dismissive but agnostic. He knows that strange things have happened and will go on happening, but he also knows he must keep his distance, lay them to one side and stick to the well-trodden path of what is known to be probable. Such alleged events cannot be caught in his net unless they float on the sea of fact, well packed round with substantial testimony. The odder and more unusual things are said to be, the more testimony is to be sought. That the general had breakfast before going into battle might be accepted, for having breakfast is something which often happens. That the general saw a vision assuring him of victory might not be accepted, for having visions is not something which often happens. 'Yes,' agrees the historian, 'some such strange thing might have happened while the commonplace thing of having breakfast might not have happened. It is just that as historian

I cannot take account of such out of the ordinary things without extra substantial witness.' It is really a very common-sense approach and one which we all use when confronted by the friend who says he has seen a ghost or a pink elephant.

But from this we can see what particular problems are raised in our search for what 'really happened' in Palestine. These stories come liberally adorned with improbable super-natural happenings for which there is no evidence that would stand up in a court of law. 'Jesus worked miraculous cures, you say! Well, you would say that, would you not, because you want to persuade me that he is the very Son of God.' Without prejudging whether such cures happened or not, it is quite proper to lay them to one side in our search for the sort of 'fact' that can be caught by the historian's net. We shall be wise to start out equipped only with what is generally judged to be probable. But I emphasise 'start out' for our notion of what is probable may be altered in the light of judgements we make on the basis of this evidence. Jones tells me he saw a pink elephant when he came out of the Bull and Bush last night. 'A likely tale,' we say. It is easily explained in terms of Jones's well-known drinking habits. Yet further information might come to light. We hear that last night an elephant escaped from a nearby circus, and round the corner from the pub we see for ourselves a collapsed ladder and an upturned pot of paint. We must at least admit that the probability of Jones's claim has been enhanced. Strange though it might be – it could have happened. The point is that probability is a necessary but rough guide. Probabilities are not iron laws, they can change. Thus if we were to conclude that our meagre hard core of evidence at least pointed in the direction of the Christian understanding of Jesus, that here indeed is the incarnate Son of God, then our view of what might have happened in such a unique life would also radically change. In the presence of him who is true God and true man, impossibilities might become possi-bilities, the effects might be quite remarkable.

Looking behind the gospel portrait

Provided we bear in mind the committed standpoint of the evangelists, the varied nature of the material they use to communicate their understanding of Christ, and provided we are aware of the limitations of historical investigation, I believe it is possible for the inexpert to look for traces of the Jesus of history; to peer behind the apostolic portrait of Christ and catch some glimpse of the one who sat for the portrait. He may judge for himself whether the Christian understanding of Jesus is required by the evidence or whether it falsifies it. As a purely practical exercise I recommend a quick reading of St Mark, the first gospel to be written, and then to ask yourself what sort of overall impression you have been given. I guess that it might turn out something like this: Here is a lay teacher, a non-professional, come from Galilee, the least religious part of Israel. He is, in all respects, a bit of an outsider. Yet with extraordinary confidence he sets about announcing what he calls the Good News of the kingdom of God. He says that this kingdom, of judgement and mercy, is coming near. It is crisis time for Israel, for the rule of God himself is just round the corner. It is time to wake up and react by a radical change of life. His teaching crackles with a sense of the holiness of God and is yet expressed in the homeliest of stories; of unemployed workers, of the late-night visitor waking the family, of lost housekeeping money, of farmers going about their work.

His words are thus both awe-inspiring and heart warming. They are also spoken with extraordinary lack of inhibition. The Man of Nazareth handles traditional hallowed teaching with breathtaking boldness. This is particularly true of his attitude to Sabbath observance: 'The Sabbath', he claims, 'is made for man and not man for the Sabbath' (Mark 2:27). And yet he is something more original than a rather boring rebel riding roughshod over the rules. He actually spends a lot of time referring back to traditional teaching but then claims to be interpreting it as God meant it to be interpreted – a much more startling business than breaking rules! In fact what astonished people was that he taught them 'as one who had authority, and not as the scribes' (Mark 1:22). For all the homeliness and warmth of his stories, his words yet bore an awful steel-like quality. This is seen in the way his words explode into action. He does not just teach the forgiveness of God but sets about to announce that forgiveness himself: 'My son, your sins are forgiven,' he says (Mark 2:5). And that is not just a startling statement; it is embodied in that welcome to his table fellowship which he extends with deliberate care to taxgatherers and sinners. Indeed, although we have tried to lay to one side reference to the miraculous, we are hard put to maintain such abstinence, and have to admit that the accounts of this teaching seem inseparable from stories of healings and exorcisms. These are seen not merely as wonders but as evidence of the newness of his teaching: 'What is this? A new teaching! With authority he commands even the unclean spirits, and they obey him.' (Mark 1:27).

Although the Man of Nazareth does not speak about himself but always points away to God and his rule, we cannot escape the fact that he sees what he is saying and doing as intimately bound up with that divine rule. The kingdom seems to come near through his teaching and his activity so that the judgement of God will depend on how people have responded or failed to respond to it. 'Truly I say to you, there is no one who has left house or brothers or sisters or mother or father or children or lands for my sake and for the gospel, who will not receive a hundredfold now in this time . . . and in the age to come eternal life' (Mark 10:29–30). Indeed as the story progresses the destiny of the kingdom seems more and more bound up with the destiny of this Man of Nazareth. What he says and does may attract crowds but it also attracts opposition – almost from the outset in Mark's gospel where we read in Chapter 3 that the Pharisees 'held counsel with the Herodians against him, how to destroy him' (Mark 3:6). While drawing the poor and the outcast, he is quickly seen as a threat to established religion and public order. So he tells the story of the vineyard owner who lets out his property to tenants. When the time comes for him to receive his proper share of the produce, he despatches servants. They are resisted and beaten up, some are even murdered. At last comes the climax, the dramatic decision to send, not servants, but 'a beloved son' who is received not with deeper respect but renewed fury. The 'beloved son' is killed and thrown out of the vineyard (Mark 12:1–8). Without argument or ringing claims the Man of Nazareth has placed himself in a category above God's servants the prophets, as the Son and heir. The story has the same explosive implications as that almost throw-away line which claims that men and women will be judged by how they have responded to this same 'beloved Son': 'whoever receives me, receives not me but him who sent me' (Mark 9:37). As stern historians in search of hard 'facts' we may lay aside stories of the baptism or transfiguration of Jesus as supernatural propaganda, and yet find on our hands material which as stubbornly insists: 'This is my beloved Son.' The question still presses: 'What is it that allows Jesus to pray to the holy mystery of God with that startling intimacy: *Abba*, Daddy, Father (Mark 14:36) and act in that Father's name with divine boldness?'

By laying to one side any heightening of the supernatural or those titles ascribed to Jesus by the evangelists, whose meaning is often elusive and controversial, we have yet in the sparsest of material this impressionistic glimpse of one whose relationship to the mystery of God seems uniquely close. We have enough, I believe, to judge whether or not the Christian community's portrait of Jesus is faithful to the original. Is the affirmation 'true God and true man' the proper flowering or distortion of this tiny seed? At least this shadowy figure connects with our questions and concerns. Does our human instinct that nothing matters more than people provide a hook into which the Man of Nazareth seems to fit? We can take this life, this piece of the human jig-saw puzzle, and see whether it will fit, and whether by fitting it makes sense of a fundamental area of our experience.

6

The Victorious Victim

The central, and unavoidable, image of Christianity is the crucifix, the man hanging on the gallows. It seems repulsive and morbid. In one village sensitive churchpeople proposed that the figure of the crucified set over the war memorial should be removed. It was deemed an unsuitable sight for children emerging from the local primary school. However sturdier members of the British Legion, knowing that this crude image reflected the realities of war, objected.

There are other ways of softening the visual offence of the crucified: the figure can be removed to leave a bare cross or dressed up in ecclesiastical robes with the marks of nails reduced to tiny scratches. Such actions can be justified. The empty cross is said to be a better image of the risen Christ and this priestly one reigning as a king shows the cross as the place of true glory. Yet these softened images are more esoteric, more withdrawn from the reality of human tragedy. Advocates of cheerful religion, eager to eradicate its sombre side, forget that it is often the tears of faith which connect with our experience. By insisting that funerals should be 'happy' occasions, with sombre hymns about judgement and black vestments banished, they repress our tears and dodge an essential part of life. We are no longer allowed to mourn over those we love. At the purely human level this is inadequate. Darkness evaded and not come to terms with, drives the pain into the background there to acquire an awful hidden power. Religiously it is inadequate. A faith which speeds through the idyllic days of Galilee to the Easter garden, with Good Friday missed out, is a faith trivialised, turned into opium of the people, a way of escape.

Faith faces the darkness

Of course we want to shut out this ghastliness and purchase peace of mind by closing our eyes to the world's pain. 'What the eye don't see the heart don't grieve about.' We have enough ways of keeping reality at bay without religion joining in this game of evasion by dosing us with gallons of synthetic joy. 'We fight for more than Love or Pleasure; there is Truth. Truth counts, Truth does count.' These words come from E. M. Forster's novel, *A Room with a View* (p. 218), which is all about the need for truthfulness in genuine human relationships. In the same way art has to be truthful even if this makes it appear harsh, raw and demanding. The bedroom farce, the jolly jingle, the chocolate-box painting, may be titillating and entertaining, but they are not art. They offer escape, in small doses, quite harmless; but they cannot claim to provide deeper insight into the way life really is. What the censorious and easily scandalised fail to recognise is that there is often more morality and godliness in the harsh, violent novel than in the sanitised thriller or sentimental novelette. 'Truth counts, Truth does count.'

To be truthful religion too must enter the darkness and face the fact of evil. It is the rugged cross which connects. The church stripped, bleak and bare on Good Friday speaks to us. The heart-rending *Agnus Dei* of a great mass is often its most accessible passage. Though religious cheerfulness in short bursts may lift the heart, an endless diet of it becomes cloying and sickly. Joy which is substantial and enduring is that which wells up through our tears. The Russian Contakion for the Departed has extraordinary power just because joy does not lie on its surface but breaks through its mournful solemnity. Christmas and Easter bells ring out with greater excitement when they have been silenced through Advent and Lent. True religion is that which bears the marks of the passion and is thus able to touch the hearts of those who are haunted by the ghastliness of the world.

The problem of evil

I shall deal first with the ghastliness, this fact of evil, in the general sense of all that threatens, diminishes or destroys human fulfilment. This includes poverty, injustice and suffering which can be traced back to some identifiable human wickedness, indifference or folly; and other ills like earthquake, famine and disease for which, it seems, we can find no one to blame. It is all this which casts its dark shadow over the world. Then I shall focus on 'sin', which is only applicable where people are culpable but which faith sees as the heart of the problem.

A problem of faith's own making

We call this burden of evil a 'problem'. But why? If life has no overall meaning, if there is no God, then it is an unpleasant threatening reality, to be eliminated if possible, but surely hardly a 'problem', save in the superficial sense of a car that has a problem starting in the morning. But when we talk about 'the problem of evil', we mean more than that. We feel indignant that things should be like this and not otherwise. We believe we are faced with some sort of contradiction. Now why should we be indignant with a set-up which may hand out earthquake and disease one minute and beautiful sunsets and mellow summer days the next? Set in a world in which pain and death are as much part of the evolutionary process as health and life, this should be the expected mixture. The path of wisdom would be to eliminate as much of the former as possible and, for the rest, to take what life hands out with stoic fortitude.

Evil as a fundamental 'problem' exists only when we see it at odds with some overall benign purpose. It is sharpened to its most acute point where we claim this benign purpose to be that of an all-loving and good God. If God has said 'yes' to this set-up, pronounced it to be 'very good', why is so much evil mixed up in it? How could God permit so much contradiction of his purposes? We need to be clear about this: evil as a problem, though not of course as an unpleasant fact, could be easily eliminated by ceasing to believe in the assertions that the world makes sense or that a good God is its creator. By abandoning faith we could extricate ourselves from the difficulty into which faith has got us in the first place. Far from 'solving' the problem of evil, faith seems to have made a rod for its own back.

A simplistic and disastrous solution

It is certainly true that believers have tried to solve the problem in simplistic and disastrous ways. Suffering has been seen as punishment for the breaking of God's laws and prosperity the reward for keeping them. While the ungodly get their just deserts, wealth and health will be the marks of the godly. This theory, of immense comfort to the affluent and successful, has had a long life and, in our own day, something of a revival. So there are modern evangelists who say that prayer can increase purchasing power and are only too eager to hail AIDS as divine punishment for sexual permissiveness. Of course this theory breaks down in face of the facts. Many good people suffer while the wicked flourish as the green bay tree. Haemophiliacs may die of AIDS while dubious characters who have made a 'killing' on the Stock Exchange possess yachts in tax havens.

The demolition of a solution

This simplistic solution in fact creaked, groaned and was broken in the book of Job. Job suffers loss of wealth, health and family. No one could be more ground down, more the victim of life's ills than he. Religious friends recite to him the traditional argument that such suffering must be evidence of sin. Instead of stubbornly protesting his innocence, he is advised to search his conscience more rigorously. Yet Job goes on arguing his own integrity not only to his friends but with astounding forthrightness to God himself. God gives his answer out of the whirlwind and it is a bleak one. Job is simply overwhelmed with the mysteriousness of life, cut down to size and made to see the littleness of his own understanding. The one who cannot bind the chains of the Pleiades or loose the cord of Orion cannot expect to unravel all life's puzzles (Job 38:31). Shall the fault-finder contend with the Almighty? What can Job say but, 'I have uttered what I did not understand, things too wonderful for me, which I did not know . . .

therefore I despise myself.' But that is not the end of the story. God rebukes the simplistic solutions of Job's comforters, and judges that it is Job, his suffering servant, who has spoken right. He may have underestimated mystery but he has retained his integrity.

The vocation of the suffering servant

Insight into the problem is further deepened in the latter part of the book of Isaiah. Israel has lived through national disaster, Jerusalem has fallen, the Temple has been destroyed and the cream of the people are now in exile. Out of this experience of national failure and suffering, a prophet speaks. What does the true servant of God now look like? Not one crowned with health, wealth and success but 'despised and rejected by men, a man of sorrows and acquainted with grief' (Isa. 53:3). Such suffering, far from being a punishment for sin, is rediscovered as a creative vocation; through it something mysterious but of great importance is being done for others. 'Surely he has borne our griefs and sorrows.' If, like Job's comforters, the outsiders of the pagan world see the battered people of God 'stricken, smitten by God and afflicted', they are to know the truth that he was 'wounded for our transgressions, he was bruised for our iniquities; upon him was the chastisement that made us whole and with his stripes we are healed' (Isa. 53:4–5).

We should notice that there is no trace here of a theoretical answer to the problems of evil for we are told nothing about where such ills come from or why, but the sufferer is elevated from the position of the passive victim and seen to be involved in a positive life-giving work. The true servant of God is one who has plunged into this world of suffering and by his solidarity with it achieves something good for others.

The answer of human solidarity

Although those in suffering and grief cry out 'Why?' they are not in fact looking for a theoretical answer. No such answer, however neat and complete, would ease their pain. They look for healing not knowledge. On the purely human level we see this happening, not just in the obvious 'happy ever after' way of health restored and success taking the place of failure, but also in those situations where there is to be no physical healing, no return of the child who has died. Even there light comes, and it comes from those who stand by and are willing to share something of the load. It is achieved by an act of human solidarity. The initial instinct of the outsider is to distance himself from the sufferer, to remain in the light and not dare to go near that darkness which is infectious and which can trouble his own happiness and security. Oh yes, we justify this shrinking by saying that we do not wish to overwhelm the hospital patient with too many visitors or to intrude on the privacy of the bereaved's grief. To move deliberately and with sensitivity into the orbit of suffering is costly yet it is done daily by friends and good neighbours. Feeling tongue-tied and totally inadequate, they declare their solidarity with those in the darkness. The halting letter, the willingness to sit in silence – these are gestures of a readiness to touch the edges of suffering, just to be there. For all their apparent feebleness, the miracle is that these gestures bring light in a way which no neat answer to the question 'Why?' could. Those who suffer know they are, as they say, 'upheld' by such expressions of solidarity.

The divine answer in the divine solidarity

God's answer to the problem of evil is of this practical nature. It is the answer of doing something about it and not the answer of theoretical knowledge. At the level of the latter his answer to Job remains: 'Face the fact of mystery that, with all your cleverness, you do not and cannot see the full picture of life as I see it. You do not see how I can weave apparent failure and waste into my final tapestry.'

Certainly false solutions must be ruled out. Suffering cannot be seen as a punishment for sin. Of those who had been cruelly massacred by Pilate and of the victims of the collapse of a tower, it was asked, 'were they worse sinners than any others?' and Jesus replied bluntly, 'No' (Luke 13:1–5). Furthermore whatever of creativity can be discovered in suffering, it is not be acquiesced in as something of its nature

87

ennobling. If we have been fortunate enough to see character enhanced by suffering, we have to admit also that we have seen it eroded and diminished. Jesus, by his ministry of healing, does not encourage passive resignation in the face of suffering. Indeed he sees himself as the man of violence plundering Satan's domain and setting free those in bondage. Stories of healing and exorcisms feature too strongly in his ministry to allow that suffering is anything other than an evil to be overcome. On meeting a man born blind the disciples ask Jesus, 'Who sinned, this man or his parents, that he was born blind?' Jesus replies, 'It was not that this man sinned or his parents', and then goes on to show that the blindness is there only to be overcome. It was 'that the works of God might be made manifest in him. We must work the works of him who sent me' (John 9:1–3).

Yet the mightiest of these works of God was shown in the crucifixion when the hands of Jesus, which had been active to heal, were riveted in impotence and he himself had become the co-sufferer, the victim. God had not simply touched the edges of suffering but had gone to its very centre. For a short period Jesus had proclaimed the kingdom and his words had been translated into those deeds which brought that kingdom near. He had worked that people should have life and have it abundantly. But his free and easy ways of loving had stirred up opposition. He is arrested and condemned to death. And it seems a tragic end to a life full of promise, another example of the worldly wisdom that, if you stick out your neck too far for ideals, you will lose your head. The puzzle is how the day of such an archetypal tragedy can be celebrated as 'Good' Friday, how this crucified man, a figure of weakness and folly, could be called 'the power of God and the wisdom of God' (1 Cor. 1:24), how his followers can insist that the victim is truly victorious. You have only to glance at the gospels to see what store the evangelists set on this event, devoting to it a disproportionate amount of their terse, economic writings. Indeed they seem to represent the whole life of Jesus as orientated towards this end, to suggest not only that Jesus was aware that his work would end in rejection and death, but that he had himself discerned that it was part of the Father's plan for him. Certainly the apostle Paul sees Christ's death as the climax of his work. Healing miracles he totally ignores and will only glory in what he sees as the mysteriously 'healing' cross (Gal. 6:14); 'we preach Christ crucified' (1 Cor. 1:23).

God as the victim

> Blest Tree, whose happy branches bore
> The wealth that did the world restore;
> The beam that did that body weigh
> Which raised up hell's expected prey.
> (Venantius Fortunatus)

Initially it seems repulsive thus to celebrate the instrument of vicious torture but if we see it as the place of God's answer to the problem of evil then we acquire the perspective which makes this possible. Healing and creativity come through God's solidarity with suffering humanity, through his becoming himself the victim.

Way back in the Old Testament, in the prophet Hosea, we already glimpse something of this divine solidarity. There God is seen not looking in from outside the human scene, sending in messages of comfort and encouragement, but as the one involved in the life of his people, bearing himself the hurt of their rejection:

When Israel was a child, I loved him and out of Egypt I called my son. The more I called them, the more they went from me; they kept sacrificing to the Baals and burning incense to idols. Yet it was I who taught Ephraim to walk, I took them in my arms and they did not know that I healed them. I led them with cords of compassion, with bonds of love and I became to them as one who eases the yoke on his jaws and I bent to them and fed them. (Hos. 11:1–4)

The picture is of God, not as the remote manipulator of plague, pestilence and famine but as infinitely close, bound up in the bundle of life with his people.

What then does the event of the crucifixion add to this, other than providing a dramatic illustration of its truth? It adds that the prophetic insight is made fact, an idea is translated into worldly reality, the Word is made flesh. Here indeed God is present sharing in human suffering as a human being. We may want to speak of God's co-suffering, his compassion, but we know that the infinite cannot suffer as the finite does. It is possible to fall into the same sort of 'pathetic fallacy' which characterises our tendency to make animal suffering in the image and likeness of human suffering. We have to continue to speak of the 'impassibility' of God because we recognise that the one who is neither tied by time nor encased by space cannot suffer like us. As the creator God is of course always close to us, involved in our every action, in him we live and move and have our being, but for him to suffer as we suffer, he must indeed step into our shoes, and so become able as a human being, set in one place and at one time, to share human pain, to endure the lonely fear of Gethsemane, to be threatened by despair as well as pain on Calvary. Here alone the 'compassion', the suffering-with, of God is more than a metaphor to be severely qualified. He has become part of the history of our race, one bit of the sum total of genuinely human experience.

The figure of the crucified thus connects with our suffering world and brings healing to our condition. The cross reflects the horrors of AIDS, brutal and sudden death, torture, cancer, and it carries to victims the good news that God himself has been right in the thick of all this as the fellow victim, the co-sufferer. There is no valley of the shadow so dark as to be empty of God. He has passed this way before us and knows what it is like. He has been the 'good neighbour' who has provided the 'answer' by being there at the deepest level, showing the most radical solidarity.

Christian community as the agent of God's solidarity

This truth cannot simply be spoken. Words are not enough, so the Christian community has to ensure that the Word made flesh is not dissolved back into mere words. Christ, in the humanity of his people, has to go down again and again into the depths, there to be exposed to sadness and horror, to be where his brothers and sisters suffer injustice, disease and deprivation. This community, which is startlingly called the body of Christ, cannot insulate itself from the pain of the world. To preach Christ crucified it has to be a sacrament of his presence in the darkness 'completing what is lacking in Christ's afflictions' (Col. 1:24).

This immersion in things human constitutes the real dignity of the 'royal priesthood' of the people of God. Those who seek to affirm this dignity often do so by encouraging lay people to capture the commanding heights of ecclesiastical life, and end by turning them into pseudo-clerics. Not only is this very dreary but it means that church machinery becomes parasitic on the world. Love and devotion are diverted from suffering humanity to the preservation of the temple. Being fully present in the world, taking things secular seriously, being the sacrament of God's continuing commitment to humanity, is what 'lay' mission is about. The same truth is witnessed to, but in a different way, by the particular ministerial priesthood of the Church. Parish priests are agents of Christ's solidarity. They do not commute from outside situations but live where they work, never handing out charity on the end of a long spoon but always serving from within. In obedience to Jesus, who is God made local, planted in the restrictions and limitations of a single human life, the parish priest falls into the soil of one given area, and through just being there earns the right to speak of the God who is there.

But suffering is not the heart of the human problem

When faith thus talks about God's solidarity in suffering it connects with our concerns, for we are desperately worried about suffering and see human fulfilment in terms of its elimination. Health education seems to offer the ultimate salvation. Colour supplements in Sunday newspapers are packed with hints for healthy eating while earnest puritans, with evangelistic fervour, denounce smoking and drinking. Doctors preach to us the merits of slimming, sweating joggers pursue their daily devotions and new ways of fasting are as commercially profitable as the sale of the old indulgences. The religious solemnity of this health religion is frequently buttressed by the *ex cathedra* pronouncements of authority figures from government and the BMA. And yet when we have jogged, dieted, given up smoking do we really look any more contented than the fat old beer-swilling countryman puffing at his pipe? 'Holiness is wholeness' has been the cry and whatever that may properly mean, we are in danger of equating holiness with healthiness, and thus making a return to a new brand of muscular Christianity.

When I was a Church of England vicar and got ground down and depressed, I would go and visit a little old crippled woman who had lain in one small room for many years. Confined to her home and deprived of most of the things which we feel to be necessary for the fulfilled life, she never allowed herself to be locked up in self-pity but radiated a happiness and interest in others which I envied. She was one of those who evidently enrich life by making something positive out of disability. I was shown that suffering is not the greatest ill nor health the greatest acquisition.

Sin – the real problem

Beneath the appalling suffering of the world, God sees to a deeper root evil, sin, which is the spurning of the love he has offered us. The rejection of love and the choice of self is the hard centre of the problem of evil. It could be that we have become tone deaf to this bleak old assertion. This does not mean we are not afflicted by bouts of guilt but that, when this happens, instead of acknowledging the disease of sin we seek easement of its symptoms. The enemy is believed to be not the offence to which the pains of remorse should have drawn our attention, but the discomfort of the pain itself. So we seek to be rid, not of sin, but of feelings of guilt. Now, of course, such feelings of guilt are not an infallible pointer to an offence. We can feel guilty of things about which we should not feel guilty at all; but more often, one suspects, we do not feel guilty when we should and this because we have become hooked on spiritual pain-killers which do not cure but suppress the sense of sin. In truth sin cannot be avoided. It is surely no accident that a culture that sets out to banish the sense of sin is a culture burdened with guilt, which sits like a monstrous load on its shoulders. Because we will not turn and face the truth, the burden becomes ever more crippling. Sin, like sex in the Victorian era, is the unmentionable subject but, again like sex in the Victorian era, very much present all the same and just because unacknowledged and hidden away, ever more destructive and dangerous.

Judgement the moment of truth

Like sin, judgement is not a popular notion. It conjures up a crude picture of the celestial lawgiver making a lot of arbitrary rules which, if broken, lead to punishment but if obeyed earn rewards. 'Thou God Seest Me' was the grim text set below the picture of a staring eye which used to look down upon my mother when, as a child, she lay huddled in the bath. But judgement is actually much more sober and simple. It is the moment of truth, a seeing how we really are, measured by that ultimate reality, God himself. It is knowing how I stand before the bar not of economic success nor of what neighbours and friends say nor of my own self-image, but before the final truth. Judgement is light showing up the fact of the matter. As such it should begin to ring bells for a generation which has set great store by authenticity and personal honesty. 'No masks for us,' we say, 'here I am as I am.' It is indeed one of the strengths of our age that we respond to E. M. Forster's words: 'We fight for more than Love or Pleasure; there is Truth. Truth counts, Truth does count.'

Jesus, says St John, is himself that light, that judgement: 'As long as I am in the world I am the light of the world. . . For judgement I came into the world that those who do not see may see, and that those who see may become blind' (John 9:5,39). In his words and deeds the light shines and people are judged by how they respond to it. Will they come out into the open and rejoice in it, or will they scuttle back into the dark hole of their own choosing? But it is in Christ's mightiest deed, his dying on the cross, that judgement reaches its climax: 'Now is the judgement of this world' (John 12:31). As Jesus stands before Pontius Pilate to be judged and condemned, the fourth evangelist shows that the roles are really reversed – Jesus is the judge and Pilate the one judged.

What is that judgement? 'I am come into the world to bear witness to the truth; everyone who is of the truth, hears my voice' (John 18:37).

The cross – the place of judgement

Calvary becomes the world's moment of truth, the place where, as St Paul puts it, 'the righteousness of God is revealed'. Measured by this righteousness we see that 'none is righteous, no not one' (Rom. 3:10). We know we have 'no excuse' (Rom. 2:1). Here a world is judged and our personal responsibility is nailed. Individuals, acting as free agents, have conspired to bring about the death of Jesus – Caiaphas and the chief priests have plotted to do away with him, Pilate has permitted an act of injustice, Simon Peter has allowed himself to be mocked into denial, individuals in the crowd have decided to open their mouths to join in the cry, 'Crucify'. This exercise of personal responsibility which we see in the passion story holds up a mirror in which we can see our own misuse of freedom in rejecting the claims of love. No, we were not there when they crucified the Lord and we should beware of dramatising our dreary and unspectacular sins by pretending that we were. And yet our solidarity with these aggressors against the incarnate God is real. In my own way, in my own situation, I have been involved in that same rejection of love which is both rejection of neighbour and God. My sin is truly laid bare by the judgement of Calvary.

Forgiveness as the breaking down of the barrier which sin erects

But what can be done about this? My sin cannot be obliterated. This I have done through my fault, my own fault, my own most grievous fault, and for ever it must remain one little part of the sum total of human events. If it is no good crying over spilt milk, yet the consequences of these acts, or failure to act, like the ripples of the stone thrown into the pond, must ever move outwards. What is done is done and the consequences are incalculable. The offence may be over and done with but its effects are very much in the present and can endure to shape the future of others besides myself. Merciful oblivion, 'just forget it', may erase it from the memory but not from the real world.

The truth is that here forgiveness, and forgiveness alone, can do something creative. This is not an act of forgetfulness; forgiving is not forgetting. Both offender and victim have to remember, have to face up to the truth of what has happened. By my offence I have set up a barrier between myself and the one I have offended. Now although the offence cannot be eradicated, the barrier built by that offence can be. The victim can refuse to allow the offence to come between us. While I erected the barrier through my failure in love, he through unwavering love, through the continued offer of friendship, can dismantle it. That is the act of forgiveness. It is not feeble indifference to what I have done but a positive creative action, which, while it cannot wipe my action off the slate, undermines its negative barrier-building power. Indeed one can go further: because in the end my sin has become the occasion of renewed and deeper love, it becomes something more than a cause for regret. Woven into the tapestry of our relationship, if always *culpa*, fault, it is now *felix culpa*, happy fault, that which through the magic touch of forgiveness is transformed into joy. It is as if a wood-carver, encountering a knot in the material on which he is working, instead of being frustrated and defeated in his purpose, accepts it and indeed overcomes it by making it part of his work of art.

Forgiveness – human and divine

In some such way do we experience forgiveness in our human relationships. So as we hear the cry, 'Father, forgive them', we recognise the voice of a brother engaged in the costliest act of barrier-breaking. 'While we were yet helpless . . . Christ died for the ungodly. Why, one will hardly die for a righteous man – though perhaps for a good man one will dare even to die' (Rom. 5:6,7). But this man, being true God as well as true man, exercises also divine forgiveness. So immediately St Paul adds that in this genuinely yet extraordinarily human action God acts 'to show his love for us' (v. 8).

The cross reveals our sin to be not only offence against our brother but also against God. The two offences are inseparably linked in this man. To fail in compassion to the needy is to fail to see the Son of God in the least of his brethren (Matt. 25:45). Falling short of love in things human I have fallen short of the love in whom we all live and move and have our being: 'He who does not love does not know God, for God is love' (1 John 4:8). Calvary is the place where humanity and God are rejected in one terrible act and so too the place of forgiveness both human and divine. The condemned one meeting brutality with love is God refusing to allow sin to be a barrier between himself and us. 'If God is for us, who is against us? . . . It is God who justifies, who is to condemn?' (Rom. 8:31,33).

That is what God is always like

But if God meets our sin like that, must it not be the case that this is how he always meets our sin? The Man of Nazareth nailed to the cross points to the very heart of God, to the Lamb slain before the foundation of the world. It is essential that this side of the truth be emphasised. The love of God we see on Calvary is nothing new but an embodiment of what is always the case. God's attitude to sinners has not changed overnight by some mysterious celestial transaction. What happened on the cross has not turned a God of wrath into a God of love. It cannot be that some 'fixed penalty' attaches to sin and has been paid by Jesus instead of by us, as a wellwisher might pay the fine of the guilty man. Bluntly we cannot conceive of a just God being indifferent as to whether the penalty is paid by the innocent or the guilty as long as it is paid. The innocent dying in place of the guilty is magnificent heroism, a sign of overwhelming love, but it can never be called the satisfaction of justice.

It is always dangerous to seize the images of faith and push them further than they are meant to go. The plucking out and over-concentration on certain images to the neglect of others is the sure way from Catholic balance to heretical lopsidedness. In no area is this more true than in our consideration of the cross. The image of the law court is used in the biblical testimony. We are indeed judged by the love for which we were created and when judged the verdict is clearly

'Guilty'. 'None is righteous, no not one . . . every mouth is stopped, the whole world held accountable to God' (Rom. 3:10,19). But the essential point of the gospel is that here the image of justice is shown to be inadequate. Just when the prisoner awaits sentence and condemnation the judge announces not that there are extenuating circumstances which permit him to impose a lighter sentence, but that the accused, for whom no excuse can be found, is acquitted and set free! The law court picture collapses. It is the same in the parable of the labourers in the vineyard (Matt. 20:1–16). There workers, irrespective of what hour they have begun to work, all get paid the same wage. 'Unfair,' we cry. But that is precisely the point – the scale of 'fairness', the wage-structure, breaks down before the divine generosity, which gives not what we deserve but what we need. In both pictures mercy, gratuitous love, goes beyond justice and fairness. If the cross is God's word written in flesh and blood, his eternal word, then it must declare what is always his attitude towards us. When Jesus, during his ministry and before his passion, declared, 'Son, be of good cheer, your sins are forgiven', he meant it. The Father's forgiveness does not have to wait upon some transaction between the eternal Son and himself.

Divine forgiveness as event – God earns the right to forgive humanly

But, if God's forgiveness does not depend on the event of Calvary, the accessibility of that forgiveness to us who live in time and space does. For us men and our salvation, what is for all eternity the case has to be made flesh in our actual history.

We may speak of God earning the right to forgive. Only as our brother can he forgive offences which are against humanity as well as against himself. Not everyone can forgive any offence. I can only forgive where I have been in some way the victim. Where I have not been the victim, no barrier has been set up between myself and the offender and thus there is no barrier to be surmounted by my continuing love. Forgiveness cannot be at second hand. There is something distasteful about comfortable middle-class intellectuals in the suburbs pretending to forgive the criminal who has mugged the old lady in the inner city. It is part of the awfulness of the Holocaust that Gentiles feel helpless before the crimes committed against Jews by a section of their Gentile world. Forgiveness can only come from the survivors of those death camps. So when a child is brutally murdered we have to be silent, allowing costly words of forgiveness to come from the parents of that child. The only carrier of forgiveness can be a victim.

Now it is true that God is always the injured party, the one whose friendship is spurned, but if the offence to be overcome is against both him and humanity, he must be part of that humanity, in solidarity with us. On the cross the divine love, which is for ever, becomes enshrined in a man, and so, by making his act of forgiveness part of our shared history, God earns the right to forgive humanly. This embodiment moreover, far from restraining the freedom of eternal love, is the only way it can be made available to us, who are inescapably enmeshed in time and space.

Making sense of difficult images

We can advance towards understanding the mystery of the crucifix along these two paths, seeing it both as God's act of solidarity with suffering humanity and as his act of forgiveness extended towards those who have rejected him and their fellow man. It has to be admitted that there are images Christians have used to illuminate the meaning of the cross which have seemed to have done the reverse. Often these images appear immoral or repulsive: Christ's death as a 'sacrifice' offered to the Father or as 'paying the price' of sin; the crucified seen as our 'substitute', standing in for us to bear the penalty of a punishing God. Nowhere do we need greater patience in continuing to pay attention to the complex Christian portrait; nowhere more do we have to rein back the impulse to be dismissive. If we would advance, we do well to edge forward, walking by the light we have already received; cling to those strong central affirmations of God's involvement in suffering and his lived-out commendation of his forgiveness, then we shall find that difficult images fall into place and bring illumination.

Substitution and paying the price

'Christ redeemed us from the curse of the law, having become a curse for us' (Gal. 3:13). Such strong mysterious words are capable of terrible distortion. I have heard an evangelist thunder: 'The lightning of the wrath of God struck Christ upon the cross instead of us.' Put that way God becomes a monster and an inwardly divided monster. But the Pauline words can point instead to the very depths of God's solidarity with the human race in its darkness and alienation – its very 'cursed' condition. God has not struck our humanity at a tangent, a superficial glancing blow, but has gone right down into the depths where we cry, 'My God, my God why hast thou forsaken me?' It is this 'going down' into the depths of our condition which is witnessed in the words of the creed: 'he descended into hell'; that is, right down to the place of silence, death and ultimate lostness.

Grasp this, the completeness of God's descent into man, and we begin to see the true meaning of the 'paying of the price'. The image is fatally stretched where some transaction is postulated – a price paid by Jesus to the Father, or even by Jesus to the devil who must have his due. The words of Peter get us thinking in the right way: 'You know that you were ransomed from the futile ways inherited from your fathers, not with perishable things, such as silver and gold, but with the precious blood of Christ' (1 Pet. 1:18,19). The picture here is of us as slaves or hostages who can only be rescued by the paying of a heavy price. What is that price? The costly enterprise of God's entry into our dereliction and death. The image finds its proper place in showing that there can be no forgiveness on the cheap.

Sacrifice

But what are we to make of the death of Jesus seen as a 'sacrifice'? The imagery is drawn from that savage world of sacrifice which offends a generation particularly sensitive to gratuitous animal suffering. However this is also a generation less dismissive of the actions of those who used to be called 'primitive', more willing to admire and learn from what seem

to be less sophisticated cultures. We may at least then be able
to tune into the instinct which, out of joy or guilt, feels the
need to give to God and to give only what is most valuable.
What is offered by the poor bedouin in the slaughter of the
best sheep in the flock is a substantial chunk of his economic
assets, the equivalent of a broker on the floor of the stock
exchange burning to the glory of God a pile of share
certificates.

Now it was the insight of the Hebrew prophets that not
even this generosity was good enough for God: 'With what
shall I come before the Lord? . . . Shall I come before him
with burnt offerings, with calves of a year old? . . . He has
showed you, O man, what is good, and what does the Lord
require of you but to do justice and love kindness and to walk
humbly with your God?' (Mic. 6:6,8). The true worshipper
is the one who offers to God nothing less than his whole self,
the one who is bent on doing what is right. The only sacrifice
ultimately worth anything is the offered life. So the Epistle to
the Hebrews sees Jesus as both the true worshipper and the
real sacrifice. He has done what we have failed to do: 'When
Christ came into the world God said, "Sacrifices and offerings
thou hast not desired, but a body hast thou prepared for
me; in burnt offerings and sin offerings thou hast taken no
pleasure." Then I said, "Lo I have come to do thy will, O
God" ' (Heb. 10:5–7). This living out of justice, mercy and
truth in the life of Jesus is the sacrifice which God has
required. Here is the true worship, the proper response of
man to the overwhelming mercy of God.

The event of the crucifixion cannot be divorced from the
life of Jesus, for what gives value to the cross is not simply a
death or a quantity of suffering. Many were cruelly put to
death in the same way but it is only in this one that we see
that particular creativity which we call 'redemption'. Jesus
made of his whole life an offering to the Father, eager to do
not his own will but the will of the one who had sent him.
All his life had been a living godwards, all was an enactment
of the prayer: 'not my will but yours'. The cross is not the
dead-end but the climax of this given-away life, where in
giving himself to the Father through death, he gives his all.
On Calvary Jesus seems just the passive victim, on the

receiving end of what a brutal system does to him. What turns the cross into the supremely creative act, is that he does not just endure but seizes the negativity and passivity and makes of it the supreme and complete self-giving. At the Last Supper Jesus had seen that his opponents were closing in on him, the inevitability of the end; and there he takes hold of what will happen and makes of it a gift which is simultaneously to the Father and to us. The cross is marked both by the dedication, 'Father into thy hands I commend my spirit', and by 'This is my body which is given for you'. The passion, what is suffered, is transformed into action, the victory of the victim. 'No one takes (my life) from me, but I lay it down of my own accord' (John 10:18).

If 'sacrifice' is the image which demands that we connect Calvary with the life lived before it, it is also the one which demands that we connect with all that happens afterwards, the passing to life of the crucified one in the resurrection and the coming to life of his followers at Pentecost. For the sacrifice of himself which Jesus offered was the sacrifice required of us all, which we had failed to make. We might have managed token gifts to God but we did not manage to make ourselves gifts to him and to our fellows. The sacrifice of Jesus is not 'instead of' or 'in place of' the sacrifice which God requires of humanity and in this sense certainly not a 'substitute'. We are not let off the hook by Jesus for it is precisely this living outwards from ourselves, making life a gift, which constitutes our human fulfilment. God's purpose is not achieved by the single triumph of the New Adam, or real man, with us still deprived of this fulfilment. So we must insist that the sacrifice of the prototype man is not instead of us but in order that we should share in the fulfilment which is his. He is not the substitute but the enabler. Thus his word to us is: 'If any man would come after me, let him deny himself and take up his cross and follow me. For whoever would save his life will lose it; and whoever loses his life for my sake and the gospel's will save it' (Mark 8:34–35). He says to us what he said to the sons of Zebedee: 'The cup that I drink you will drink; and with the baptism with which I am baptised, you will be baptised' (Mark 10:39).

To talk of how we are caught up in that perfect love which

was lived out in Palestine is to be pointed through the Easter garden to the rebirth of the community of his friends and followers. However St John, who wants to bring out the intimate connection between cross, resurrection and sending of the Holy Spirit, makes the place of the rebirth of the community the foot of the cross. Here the followers of Jesus are given to one another, Mary his mother to the beloved disciple and the beloved disciple to Mary (John 19:26). Here too this community of love is assured that it will be given a share in the fulfilled life which is the sacrificed life, through water and blood, the sacraments of baptism and the Eucharist, which flow from the pierced side of the crucified (John 19:34). We may thus, with St John, anticipate and touch upon ways in which Calvary comes alive and impinges upon us.

Once for all and ever new

Christianity moves between two poles. On the one hand it insists that the crucifixion was an event, something which happened in time under Pontius Pilate. Unlike a myth or edifying story, the cross does not float above history but is truly part of it and thus unrepeatable. Jesus 'has no need to offer sacrifice daily . . . he did this once for all when he offered up himself' (Heb. 9:27). On the other hand it is insisted that what happened nearly two thousand years ago touches our lives in the twentieth century as much as those of Simon Peter and his friends. The act of God's forgiveness is not locked in the past but reaches down the ages.

Eucharist – the living sacrifice

According to St Paul (1 Cor. 11:23ff), when Jesus took bread at the Last Supper and pronounced the mysterious words, 'This is my body', he added, 'Do this in remembrance of me.' This act of 'remembrance' has continued ever since. Before ever the pages of the New Testament were written it was going on, and wherever Christians have assembled and at whatever time, it has gone on. 'Was ever another command so obeyed?' asks Dom Gregory Dix in his great work on *The Shape of the Liturgy* (p. 744).

This act of remembrance has always been seen as something more than a sign, like a war memorial, set up to stir memories of a past event. The Last Supper, whether a Passover meal or not, is firmly set within the context of the Jewish Passover. This for the people of Israel is more than a looking back in time; it is rather the past invading the present so that the faithful today can claim their share in the liberating event of the Exodus. So St Paul insists that this 'doing in remembrance' proclaims the Lord's death until he comes (1 Cor. 11:26). Very early on in the life of the Christian Church, the language of sacrifice which had been applied to the cross was taken and applied to the eucharistic meal (for example, Didache, 14). This was not another sacrifice, necessary because the sacrifice of Calvary was thought to be incomplete, nor was it a repetition of Calvary, but it was a making present, a focusing for us of that offering of the Son to the Father which had been enfleshed once in space and time. Here the one true sacrifice, Jesus himself, the same yesterday, today and for ever, is made known in the breaking of the bread (Luke 24:30,31).

So when we come before God, and that sure primitive instinct stirs to offer to him only what is most precious and worthy, we find our hands empty and ask: 'What have we the human race really to offer?' Only the Man, the one true and complete member of our race, who lived and died true humanity in Palestine all those years ago. It is as if we say: 'As you the Holy One look on your children – look first on Jesus, your Son indeed, in whom your image shines as brightly as it should. He is the best our world has to offer.' But this does not let us off the hook, it does not mean, 'Look on him instead of us. Accept his offering in place of ours.' He is our brother. We can be joined to him, be in solidarity with him, as taxgatherers and sinners entered his friendship through the shared meal. We are able to be caught up in that same movement of divine love expressed once upon a time in our humanity by Jesus. With him we can offer ourselves, our souls and bodies to be a living sacrifice (Rom. 12:1).

The living word in the sacrament of reconciliation

If the cross 'comes alive' in the Eucharist, it also 'comes alive' when the words of the Christian community become a sacrament through which God continues to make the appeal of the cross, 'be reconciled' (2 Cor. 5:20). This appeal of the living word is made in the most direct and personal way through the sacrament of reconciliation. Here the generalised sense of there being a barrier between the holy God and sinful man becomes the recognition of that barrier which by my own offences I have erected between myself and God. It is no longer all up in the air, a matter of generalisations, but utterly personal, direct and concrete. My confession is a dreary enough shopping list of sins but in its particularity I cannot escape into that vague sense of unease which in fact is no escape but the way to acquire a destructive sense of guilt. This is my moment of truth when I see myself measured by the love of God. I can no longer evade personal responsibility.

This attempt to be honest before God takes place, not by myself, but in the presence of the priest who, as he communicates the forgiveness of God (John 20:23), acts as the representative of the Christian community and mankind which I have injured. This is neither a wallowing in guilt nor a religious version of psychoanalysis, it is for the sake of reconciliation with God and my brothers and sisters. In the confessional the forgiveness of God becomes as particular and real for me as that dreary list of sins. God is forgiving THIS me of THESE sins. Through the earthen vessel of his priestly minister, Christ says once again: 'Son, be of good cheer, your sins are forgiven.'

7

Flame in the Night

On Easter day words fail us. Sermons seem to waver between euphoric mumbo-jumbo and a banal insistence that to every cloud however dark there is a silver lining. The former makes us feel that we have been ushered into a never-never land of unreality and the latter that nothing has really been added to the world we know only too well. Certainly Easter abounds with heady imagery. 'Christ is risen! We are risen!' we sing. But are we? In the daffodil-adorned church the illusion of newness may be induced, but come the end of the holiday we are back with the grey unsatisfactoriness and boredom of the old world. What price new creation now? There is a problem. While the crucified one inhabits the real world his alleged resurrection seems to lift him out of it. Easter feels like wishful thinking, the mythological icing of a 'happy ever after' ending slapped on to the tired old fruit cake of reality. Unlike the cross the empty tomb does not connect with our experience. We suspect that we have been taken for a ride by Christian cheerfulness.

The restraint of the Easter stories

In fact the gospel accounts of the resurrection themselves contain an element of reserve and restraint. There is overwhelming joy and no inhibition in the desire to share that joy. Yet joy is not purchased on the cheap. It is frankly recognised that the good news of Christ risen is not a public event but a secret which came initially to a faithful few. All the outside world has to go on is an empty tomb to be inspected and the strangely excited followers of the executed Jesus. The former could be explained away by assuming that his missing body had been stolen, and the latter either by deceitful fanatacism or, more likely, wishful thinking so intense that it exploded into hallucination. Whatever had happened was not open to inspection by a detached commission of enquiry. It seemed only accessible to those who, despite hesitation and desertion at the last, had thrown in their lot with Jesus. The gospels seem frank about this. Moreover the evangelists make it clear that the brutal reality of Calvary is not bypassed or swept away by whatever happened in that garden; the suffering and death of Jesus are not cancelled out. He comes to the disciples bearing in his hands and side the marks of his passion.

Reserve and restraint thus seem to be part and parcel of the authentic Easter gospel. Indeed where the words of preachers fail the liturgy seems to succeed, and manages to communicate this strange blend of joy welling up through a darkness which yet remains real. On the eve of the feast Christians assemble in a dark and silent church. Fire is lit. The risen Christ, light of the world, is proclaimed, and from this burning fire a single large candle is carried into the church. As that point of light makes its way through the darkness it becomes contagious, for from it candles held by those assembled are lit. The effect is of intense drama and also real restraint. The dark shadows of the church still press in upon us and the flickering candlelight seems so vulnerable. Yet the pool of light is a growing one becoming an ever more substantial opponent of the darkness.

The realism of Easter faith

This liturgy seems exactly to express hope without trivialising the reality of the darkness. Easter brings no escape from suffering and death. The last enemy is still with us and, in company with Jesus, each individual has to pass through this valley. For the world there is no escape from injustice, war, grinding poverty, famine and disease. No magic wand has been waved to banish these things, no divine recipe handed out for their instant solution. The post-Easter world is still in the hands of frail, confused, sinful people like ourselves who have to use minds and energy to wrestle with its ills. From this continuing human task no being 'born again' with Jesus can rescue us; not even sanctity is a substitute for wise political decision.

Faith has witnessed to this realism in a number of ways. The devil, it is said, has received a mortal blow but, dangerous as any wounded beast, still goes about seeking whom he may devour (1 Pet. 5:8). Wariness as much as hope is a Christian virtue. To put it another way, we may in the light of Easter be enjoying the firstfruits, a foretaste of the harvest, but the harvest itself is not yet come. As Gregory the Great writes: 'Dawn announces that night has already passed, but it does not display the full brightness of day; while it is dispelling the one it is welcoming the other, and it keeps light and darkness intermingled' (*Commentary on the Book of Job*, 29. 2–4). St Paul takes seriously the 'groaning' of all creation, a 'groaning' shared even by those who have 'the firstfruits of the Spirit'. Here and now we live in hope: 'In this hope we were saved. Now hope that is seen is not hope. For who hopes for what he sees? But if we hope for what we do not see, we wait for it with patience' (Rom. 8:22–25). Instead of being in the happy position of having arrived at the heavenly city we are still pilgrims on the way. In such varied images faith resists euphoric triumphalism and bears witness to that strand of restraint in the Easter stories.

One should insist that this tension between greyness and glory, incompleteness and possession cannot be resolved by placing a line between the secular world and the community of faith, making the former all darkness and the latter all light. The city of God and the city of man cannot be marked out with such neatness. While in the secular city sparks of Easter light can be discerned amidst the darkness, the community of faith remains a mixed-up mixture. For all that the apostle Paul dares to call the latter the 'body of Christ', he does not use this image as a cover-up of its unsatisfactory, even scandalous nature. Neither divine grace nor the devil observes 'no-go' areas.

Greyness in politics and spirituality

Coming to terms with this continuing greyness has implications for politics and spirituality. Any utopianism which
suggests that particular political remedies can bring in the
kingdom of God is ruled out. These remedies are necessary
but must never be divinised. No pinches of incense can be
offered to the emperor however idealistic, or even Christian,
he may appear. All our human arrangements remain human
and so under the judgement and mercy of God. They are
under judgement because they always fall short of his love.
They are under mercy because even these rough and ready
attempts at justice can be steps in the direction of that love.
By so making the affairs of the city relative and not absolute,
faith, far from devaluing them, invests them with greater
seriousness. Because Christians are not allowed to sell their
souls to 'the party', they will be agents of disturbance,
appearing to be bad 'party men' yet in truth serving the party
best by never allowing it to settle into complacency. This
does not provide a charter to opt out, to become the perpetual
nagger in the wilderness; rather in being liberated from the
absolute claims of ideology the believer is made more practical, more alert to the real possibilities in any given situation.
A few faltering steps in the direction of justice and compassion
will seem to him better than the wildest of dreams.

We have also to come to terms with greyness in our spirituality. Religious 'experience', our feeling for the realities of
faith, ebbs and flows. While one day we may delight in the
sense of God's nearness, the next we may feel simply dry and
listless, our prayer reduced to a bare longing to pray, or even
a longing for that longing. Faced by this we are sometimes
encouraged to push our foot down on the accelerator and force
ourselves into renewed religious feeling. In such attempts to
bounce ourselves back on to a 'high', we may be generating
emotions which are simply unreal, and then, when we realise
their phoneyness, the state of religious depression only
increases. As I have said earlier, the great guides to prayer
are remarkably unimpressed by religious emotion, and insist
that faith, not feeling, is the real thing. Walking by faith
involves a lot of gritty plodding on in darkness with our wills

like the bed of the sea over which the waters of emotion swirl, the solid base which has yet little control over the turbulence. But it is to that deep-down rockbed of faith that God looks, not to the ebullient froth and foam of those carried by the volatile currents of feeling. God wants, not fair-weather companions but the solid friendship of those who cling on in storm, dreariness and darkness. Easter people have to be content with the frail but sure light of the candle moving through darkness rather than the blaze of light which drives away all shadows.

Resurrection – Jesus goes forward to fulfilment

The acceptance of greyness in politics and spirituality is part and parcel of this restraint of the Easter gospel, a doing justice to the fact that the scars of the risen Christ are not removed. But this recognition does not take the edge off our sense of joy and victory, it does the reverse. Were the cross taken away by Easter, we should have merely a return to Galilee, a going back to what Jesus was before Calvary. His resurrection would be simply the revival of a corpse, the prolongation of a life. And that is certainly not what the gospels proclaim. Jesus is raised up, not to go back, but to go forward. This real Jesus, the one encountered by Peter and his friends in Palestine, the one they listened to, the one they saw and touched has passed through death, not to annihilation nor to become some disembodied spirit or a lingering memory, but into the glory of God. In the picture-language of faith Jesus is raised up and seated at the Father's right hand. In other words this is Christ's journey's end: for 'true God' the coming home where he belonged; for 'true man' the fulfilment of the human task. As St John sees them, the two events we call resurrection and ascension are really parts of one movement in which the eternal Son returns to glory carrying with him that real humanity, in and through which he has, in those few years, lived out the pattern of divine love. The task of refashioning human nature to its original design is over. The work is completed.

It is important to grasp that this 'glorification', the passing of Jesus to his fulfilment, is the heart of the Easter message, compared with which his appearances to his followers are secondary. As far as God is concerned the story would be complete without any such appearances. They are given only for our sake, to reassure us that death could not in fact contain the prince of glory.

The resurrection – the setting free of love

In thus moving forward Jesus does not go from us. The real presence of 'true God and true man' is not followed by a real absence. In fact the reverse is the case for that divine love, focused under the limitations of real humanity in Palestine, is now free from restriction. In his earthly life the Son of God could, like us, do only one thing at a time. If he was healing in Capernaum he could not be healing in Jerusalem. If those in Nazareth were hearing him speak, those in Jericho could not. As truly man Jesus was restricted by time and space.

But love is of its nature impatient of such restrictions; it wants to move ever outwards, to embrace more and more. The family we most admire is the one which, stable in love, is not a self-absorbed unit but able to open its doors to welcome others. God is love, perfect and secure within himself, yet that love bursts its bounds, overflowing to embrace all creatures. God's love is by nature universal. For such love to be set down and lived out in the restraints necessary to a genuine human life is to create tension. If this is to be human love it has to accept restraints, to become particular. To love humanly is to love the neighbour, the one who is actually put in my way. There are no short cuts: if I take off into a theoretical love for all mankind I am likely to miss the needs of the man next door. It is notorious that many high-minded men, captivated by a vision of a whole world to be loved, are deficient as husbands and fathers.

Jesus as the truly universal lover does not fall into this trap, instead he accepts what is to hand and concentrates on loving those he encounters. Before his love can burst out to the Gentile world he must first carry out his mission to 'the lost sheep of the House of Israel' (Matt. 15:21–28). Indeed the gospels do not give a picture of a philanthropic campaign efficiently organised to bring the maximum benefit to the greatest number of people. In the complaints of the brothers of Jesus there is a touch of the party agent's irritation with his candidate, who seems content to bumble around the constituency knocking on doors and kissing babies when he should be focusing on those photo opportunities and TV-catching rallies for the faithful. Why hang around in insignificant Galilee? Go where the action is, make an impact, head straight for the centres of power and influence. 'Leave here and go to Judea, that your disciples may see the works you are doing. For no man works in secret if he seeks to be known openly. If you do these things, show yourself to the world' (John 7:3–4). But Jesus resists this attempt to entice him into a phoney universality. Greeks come wanting to see him. He recognises the significance of this: 'The hour has come for the Son of man to be glorified.' Indeed this glory will mean nothing less than the gathering into one of God's scattered children (John 12:20ff). But there can be no bypassing what lies to hand, no purchase of the universal at the cost of the particular. In fact the truly universal love can only be reached by that ultimate restriction which is the climax of his mission, the restraint by wood and nails, the acceptance of his sphere of influence reduced to this place of execution where love will embrace those few around him, his mother, his companions in death and his executioners. Love embraces a world by being narrowed down to this single cruel point, 'unless a grain of wheat falls into the earth and dies, it remains alone; but if it dies it bears much fruit' (John 12:24).

But what has been thus narrowed down, concentrated in the lonely victim on execution hill, now bursts forth through his rising to move from Jerusalem and Judea, to the very furthest corners of the earth. The risen Jesus is set free to love where and when he wants, at any time and in any place. 'I am with you always, even to the end of the world' (Matt. 28:20). So the resurrection is the fulfilment of the divine desire to love humanly every man, woman and child of every age. Easter makes God in the form of man totally accessible. The risen Jesus is free to be where he will, unfettered by the restrictions of time and place. As the gospels tell us locked doors cannot restrict his universal loving.

111

The heart of the Easter gospel is what happens to Jesus, his arrival at journey's end, his fulfilment, which, far from being an abandonment of this world, allows him to be present for all ages and all places in a way at once universal and uniquely personal. Love has got what love has always wanted, the homecoming which is also the voyage, the return to the Father which is, at the same time, the sending out to the furthest corners of the earth.

The appearances of the risen Christ – the signs of assurance

In this context we can understand the recorded resurrection appearances. The lingering of the risen Christ among his friends is emphasised only in the Lucan writings and the supplement to the fourth gospel (John 21). Mark provides no appearance of the risen one and simply gives the promise of a reunion in the future. At the tomb the young man says to the women: 'He is risen, he is not here; see the place where they laid him. But go and tell his disciples and Peter that he is going before you to Galilee, there you will see him as he told you' (Mark 16:3–6). And there, with the women fleeing from the tomb in trembling astonishment, Mark rings down the curtain. Matthew and John both add the appearance of Jesus in or near the garden, and later to the eleven apostles; for Matthew on a mountain in Galilee, for John in a house, presumably in Jerusalem. While John seems to extend the period of appearance to eight days, Matthew gives no time scale. It is only Luke in the Acts of the Apostles who extends the period explicitly to forty days (Acts 1:3). But whether brief and enigmatic as in Mark, or prolonged and leisurely as in the Lucan writings and the Johannine supplement, the evangelists all find a place for some communication to the friends of the risen Lord. If the heart of Easter is what happens to Jesus, his glorification or fulfilment, there has to be this pause to bring peace and joy to the disciples for Easter is not complete without the first proclamation of the Easter gospel. To doubting Thomases who cry 'Unless I see in his hands the print of the nails and place my fingers in the mark of the nails and place my hand in his side, I will not believe,' assurance is given in a way which such pragmatists can understand. St John gives a vivid picture of Jesus speeding on his way back 'home', yet pausing to share the news of his victory with those he has loved. 'Do not hold me,' he says to Mary Magdalene, 'for I have not yet ascended to the Father, but go to my brethren and say to them, I am ascending to my Father and your Father, to my God and your God' (John 20:17).

The spiritually minded become uneasy about the provision of such assurance. Is this not to do away with faith, a concession to an evil and adulterous generation which hankers after signs? So attempts are made to refine things, to render the resurrection more ethereal, a spiritual vision or something in the mind. Unfortunately for the spiritually-minded, the apostles are represented as rather gross and earthbound, those for whom seeing is believing. Indeed Jesus does say to Thomas, 'Blessed are those who have not seen and yet believe' (John 20:29), but in order to rescue the good news from becoming the private possession of the high-minded and to make it available to us who are of the earth, earthy, the evangelist immediately adds: 'Jesus did many other signs in the presence of the disciples' (v. 30). This is consistent with the Johannine teaching on the mighty actions of Jesus. They are not mere wonders. They summon us to look more carefully, to perceive the hidden spiritual depth, but their earthy nature is not ignored. For St John it is always through the material to the spiritual.

The empty tomb

To some there is no greater stumbling block than the traditional insistence on the bodily resurrection of Jesus requiring a literally empty tomb. It not only seems highly improbable but also easily explicable in terms of the well-known human tendency to dramatise events by making them seem more concrete and definite than they really were. A good tale gets embellished, 'fleshed out', as we should say. Are not the stories of the risen body and the empty tomb in truth vivid ways of expressing the continuing liveliness of the influence of Jesus of Nazareth? Indeed, it is argued, if you turn to the earliest record of the resurrection (1 Cor. 15) you will find no reference to an empty tomb. The alleged appearances of the risen Christ are seen as the same sort of experience which Saul had on the road to Damascus, a vision rather than the quasi-physical presence of one who eats before our eyes. All of which connects with what the apostle says later in that chapter about the raising of the dead: 'Flesh and blood cannot inherit the kingdom of God' (v. 50); what is 'sown a physical body is raised a spiritual body' (v. 44). As all through the chapter the resurrection of Jesus is linked with the general raising of the dead – 'if there is no resurrection of the dead, then Christ has not been raised' (v. 13) – it seems fair to conclude that, like ours will, the bones of Jesus lay in some grave, while the 'spiritual body' lives on.

My college chaplain knew an old canon of Christ Church who, whenever he visited the dentist for an extraction, would carefully preserve the tooth in a box, which was to be buried with him when he died. He was not going to arrive at the Messianic banquet without the proper equipment! Few of us hold such a vigorously physical view of the resurrection body. We do not expect tombs to fly open on the Last Day and the dead to pop out with their nicely reassembled bodies. If we have so modified our understanding of 'the resurrection of the body', why should we not do the same in our understanding of the risen Christ? Surely we are being true to the apostle Paul by thus seeing the pioneer of our faith treading the same path we are to tread.

I confess I have difficulty in getting hold of the meaning of such proposed reinterpretations of the resurrection of Jesus. What exactly is meant to take the place of the old 'bodiliness'? Is the new version, without empty tomb or Christ eating the fish, in fact another rendering of the old doctrine of the immortality of the soul, a reaffirmation that after death some indestructible spark of the divine lives on? But if this is what early Christians were trying to say it is hard to understand why they did not say it in that way. The doctrine was familiar in the Graeco-Roman world and known to Jews (Wisd. 9:15). But if that is not what the reinterpretation means, then is it that the 'spirit' of Jesus lives on, in the same way as the soul of John Brown goes 'marching on' while his body lies 'a-mouldering in the grave'; that this Man of Nazareth, like

Karl Marx, continues to be influential long after his death? Or does the Easter story state that his dispirited bunch of followers have 'come alive' with new faith and hope, so that the resurrection is their transformation and liveliness? The truth is that these explanations, which may set us free from troublesome supernaturalism, sound distinctly banal. In the first two nothing is said which could not be said more easily in other ways, and in the third we are left with a bigger puzzle than ever. If the Easter stories are the product of a community come to life, then what was it that made this happen and produce a movement so remarkably creative and influential in the history of western civilisation?

Such reinterpretations seem to betray an ideological motivation. I hear in them the voice of those who say in the name of hard-headed science that miracles do not happen; who, confronted by an alleged miracle, disdain to do the scientific thing, which is to investigate it with rigour, and, on a priori grounds, are simply dismissive: this miracle has not happened because miracles do not happen! This is as much 'faith', ideology or prejudice as that of the most credulous believer who sees miracles round every corner. It is, in Newman's words, 'an infidelity founded on presumptions on the side of unbelief as much as believers' faith is founded on presumptions on the side of belief'.

Whatever may be said for this prejudice or belief, the attempt to eliminate the supernatural by taking off, at the point where the material is said to be effected by the spiritual, into the realms of visions or new ways of looking at things, ill accords with the down-to-earthness of Jewish thinking. The Bible consistently insists that this world is the theatre of God's activity. Unless St Paul has broken with this tradition, the raising of the dead would for him inevitably mean something to do with bodies. When he distinguishes in 1 Corinthians 15 between 'physical' and 'spiritual' bodies, the element of continuity is as strong as that of discontinuity. The key image is the relationship between the seed and the fruit which grows from it. When in 2 Corinthians he faces the destruction of our 'earthly tent', he sees hope, not in the abandonment of tents altogether but in the provision of a heavenly one: 'not that we would be unclothed, but that we would be further clothed, so that what is mortal may be swallowed up in life' (2 Cor. 5:1–5).

It is I myself – the meaning of the sign

Certainly as far as the evangelists are concerned the resurrection appearances have a good deal to do with earthy 'bags of bones'. 'They came up and took hold of his feet' (Matt. 28:9). Jesus is said to have eaten a portion of broiled fish (Luke 24:43). The invitation to Thomas to feel those scarred hands is shockingly physical. While this poses all sorts of insoluble difficulties, it is not difficult to grasp the fundamental point which the evangelists were making. If we are not in a position to say what 'really' happened, in the sense of what we would have seen had we been there, we are in a position to understand what is being affirmed. The evangelists are not talking simply about the resuscitation of a corpse, a return to those days of the earthly ministry with Jesus just carrying on where he left off. This is made clear by the nuancing of the physical language. The presence of Jesus is real but it is elusive and mysterious. He who seems so solid yet vanishes and appears at will. We need to pay attention to the careful balance of the gospel witness. For a brief moment the risen Lord seems to hover between two worlds; speeding to his heavenly home, he still has a foot in this world. And why? Assuredly not for the completeness of his own glorification, but for our sake that we should know it is the real Jesus of Nazareth who lives. St Luke puts it like this: 'See my hand and my feet that it is I myself; handle me and see, for a spirit has not flesh and bones as you see that I have' (Luke 24:39).

'It is I myself' – that is the key to the appearances. The risen Jesus is not a spiritual 'bit' detached from the physical-ness through which his friends had known him, he is not the label for a bundle of ideas or ideals – he is himself, the complete person they had come to know as they walked and talked on the roads of Palestine. This is the one who has passed to glory, this the one with whom, wherever they may be, whenever they may be, they may enter into an ever deeper relationship. The time of 'the holy in the homely' continues, the 'personal centre' remains. Indeed the 'sign of assurance' is swiftly accomplished and soon his followers will not be able to depend on the manifestation of his glorified humanity, so that those will be blessed 'who have not seen yet believe' (John 20:29). However what they believe will be the same as what Peter and his friends believed, that it is the real Jesus, not some shadow of his former self, who lives on. Although there is now no 'seeing', there is still a vital dependence on what was once seen, and on the testimony of those who were able to say, 'that which we have seen and heard we proclaim also to you', of those who once cried, 'Yes, it is the Lord' (John 21:7).

The reconciliation of otherworldliness and worldliness

The witness of the evangelists binds together two human concerns which are often in conflict: a concern about what may lie beyond death and a concern to make the best of this life. Until we see otherworldliness and worldliness indissolubly united, we have not fully grasped the Easter gospel.

However much we may try to face the fact of our own impending death or come to terms with the loss of those we love, we remain in a state of rebellion against this our last enemy. We may have tried to be content with those memories of the dead which cannot be taken away. We may comfort ourselves with the thought that their influence for good can never be eradicated. But surely this belief in 'personal survival' is a selfish lust for life beyond its proper limits. We should turn from such wishful thinking to concentrate on the continuing life of the human race. Instead of looking to some heaven beyond, our concern should be the improvement of this earth in the here and now. Aided by the contributions of those who are dead, the human race struggles towards a more just and humane society. What richer immortality could there be than to have lived and died for this struggle? It seems a noble and unselfish vision.

Hope beyond death

And yet a rebellious instinct stirs within us and will not let us be satisfied. No memory of the dead, no recognition of their continuing influence can be a substitute for these unique persons we have loved and lost, for we did not love them just for their ideas, which can be remembered, nor for their actions, which can still be effective, but simply for their being themselves. It was Jack and Jill I loved, not Jack's thoughts or Jill's deeds. It was this particular smile, this expression, this gesture, this loving embrace that meant everything to me. My heart is not satisfied with the thought that they are now memories or stepping stones on the way to Utopia. It is all very well to march ever onwards towards the new Jerusalem, but come that perfect city of man, the only people who will pass through its gates will be those who happen to be alive at that time. The dead will be locked out. In fact we see around us evidence that this secular vision has results less noble than we had been led to expect. People become means to an end, individuals disposable for the sake of the great cause. The Jewish 'problem' can be solved, class 'enemies' eliminated, innocent bystanders kidnapped, threatened and murdered, all because the future of mankind seems to demand it. Despite the crocodile tears, these things are said to be sadly necessary. 'It is expedient that one man die.' In rejecting this cold creed we are affirming our belief in the ultimate value of unique individuals, that real people matter more than abstract causes, and so reflecting something of what the Second Vatican Council articulated in its insistence that: 'It is a sound instinct that makes man recoil at the thought of his total destruction, or being snuffed out. He is more than matter, and the seed of eternity he bears within him rebels against death' (*Church in the Modern World*, 18.22).

Having smiled at the elderly canon who preserved his teeth for the day of resurrection, let me now bluntly say that my heart warms more to his vigorous realism than to those thinner high-minded versions of immortality. If the rising of Jesus is more than a going back to the life he once lived on this earth, it really is more, and not less. It is a carrying forward into glory of a chunk of this earth. What the evangelists struggled to speak of is not the *less* than earthly but the *more* than earthly. In his book *The Great Divorce* C. S. Lewis makes this point. It is about an outing to heaven by some citizens of hell. These trippers from the nether regions are

118

characterised not by their grossness but by their insubstantiality, while their heavenly hosts, contrary to the expectation that their spirituality will make them well-nigh invisible, have rock-like solidity.

I once tried to explain to a young boy in Sunderland the meaning of heaven. I began by asking him what he could honestly say that he had most enjoyed in his short life. 'A trip to see the illuminations at Blackpool,' was his answer. I had no hesitation or theological qualms in saying, 'Well, heaven will be like that. Only much greater.' Human fulfilment, like the fulfilment of Jesus, has to be seen as a 'more than' not as a 'less than'. We may mock some of the traditional colourful images of the life of the world to come. Of course they are inadequate but I suspect less misleading than their depressingly spiritualised rivals, which suggest subsistence rather than existence, something less than this red-blooded life. Provided one knows that the images are always pointing towards the 'something infinitely greater' – 'What no eye has seen, nor ear heard, nor the heart of man conceived, that God has prepared for those who love him' (1 Cor. 2:9) – it seems right to see heaven in the harmony of harps and the joy of a banquet. Our journey's end is the fulfilment of all we have discovered in this life to be good.

At the heart of all the images we use to describe the indescribable, are those of Easter which speak of the personal fulfilment of Jesus in ever deeper companionship with his friends. The assurance is that beyond death we shall be fully ourselves, our personal identity will not be lost in a great sea of the divine or a regimented collective or a private heaven reached by the flight of the lone to the alone; but fully with one another in perfect love. All the loose ends and unsatisfactoriness of our present loving will find fulfilment in that love from which nothing can separate us.

Facing death – the difference the hope beyond makes

Such hope cannot but effect how we cope with the fact of death here and now. Certainly we have to come to terms with its reality and take seriously the words of our Lord to Mary Magdalene: 'Do not cling to me.' It is necessary to learn to 'let go' of the dead and not try to drag them back to this earth. The loss is real. As they have not just slipped into the next room there is discontinuity to be faced. Between the burial of Jesus on Good Friday and his rising during the night of Easter we recognise an important lull, a time of sad exhaustion, an experience of bereavement. A fully Christian funeral expresses this and so allows room for our tears and sense of loss.

As long as this 'letting-go' is taken seriously, Christians are encouraged to move forward to enter into a new and mature relationship with the dead. We learn to pray for them simply because we recognise that, whether we live or die, we are the Lord's. Together we are held in the same love of God from which 'nothing can separate us' (Rom. 8:38–39). Because Jesus has broken down the iron curtain of death, nothing can stop our obstinate loving, and so, just as we pray for our dead, we expect them to pray for us. That is not presumption or idle speculation, it is simple confidence in the reality of love which the last enemy could not conquer. In the Eucharist we affirm our belief in this continued human interdependence, referring to the saints as those 'on whose constant intercession we rely for help' (Eucharistic Prayer, 3). Instead of self-made Christians scrabbling up a ladder to avoid being beholden to anyone, we rejoice in being members one of another, allowed to bear one another's burdens. A whole dimension of true humanism was lost in the Reformation's assault on prayers for the dead and requests for the prayers of the saints. The context in which the human drama is played out was diminished and man left a lonelier creature.

The hope beyond – the difference it makes to the tasks of this world

It has to be admitted that Christians have become somewhat coy about affirming belief in life after death. Not only does it seem to be too good to be true but we fear that it may distract us from the tasks of this world. If true, it must set human problems and hopes in a radically new context. The fact that this life is not everything, that the dead are not simply snuffed out, will rescue us from the despair that counts the millions slaughtered in disasters as lives wasted. They are 'in the hands of God, and there shall no torment touch them' (Wisd. 3:1). But this is precisely where the unease arises. Does not such 'other-worldly' hope blunt the urgency of our efforts to prevent such disasters?

I believe that it does not. We labour to prevent or alleviate suffering but the truth is that our best efforts often fail or are miserably inadequate. What then are we to do? Beyond renewed efforts we tend to fall into lethargic guilt. Because we have believed that 'everything was up to us', that all depended on our skill and ability, confronted by this inevitable failure or incomplete success we are easy victims of despairing inertia. Effective and sustained action requires a certain tough-minded ability to relax; as my mother used to put it, 'do your best, and leave the rest', with confidence that this little bit is something worthwhile. It is here that otherworldliness comes to the aid of worldliness, not by adding an escape clause but by showing that every act of human love is joined to the divine movement of love, which, though using our efforts, is always stronger. The believer can make his modest contribution calmly because he knows that 'underneath are the everlasting arms', that in the end 'all things are well, all manner of things are well'.

Belief in life eternal gives to our actions in this world a new significance and seriousness. The decisions I make here and now are part of the fashioning of the 'me' that will be judged by the burning fire of God's love. We are taught that our final destiny is fixed by whether we spot the beggar Lazarus at the gates; by whether we have served the incognito Christ in the hungry, imprisoned and naked.

Hope which invades the here and now

The value which the risen Christ sets on this world is to be seen not only in what he demands but also in what he gives. The New Testament is clear that the new life which he comes to share with us cannot be banished to some remote hereafter, it touches this earth here and now. Already 'we have been called out of darkness into God's marvellous light' (1 Pet. 2:9); already 'we have been raised up with Christ' (Col. 3:1); 'If anyone is in Christ, he is a new creation, the old has passed away, behold the new has come' (2 Cor. 5:17). This 'newness' is not treated as something purely spiritual or in the mind, it makes a difference in this world. The life of Jesus, says St Paul, is 'manifested in our mortal flesh' (2 Cor. 4:11).

On that Easter morning 'what the disciples were looking at was the first day of the new creation' (G. K. Chesterton, *The Everlasting Man*), and what we celebrate in our annual vigil is nothing less than the transformation of the possibilities of this life. Of course the candle still struggles against the encroaching darkness. This new life is a small hidden fragile thing, but it is as effective as disinfecting salt or yeast in the dough. Real life is open to real changes. If God takes us as we are he yet does not leave us as we are. His love is creative, able to make us more than we are. Human beings can become saints, those who in their precious uniqueness are conformed to the image of Christ.

Yet this newness, although focused in the community of faith and supremely in the lives of the saints, is not locked up here. A world, not just a church, has been redeemed. The new life is to be discovered here, there and everywhere, for the spirit of the age to come bloweth where it listeth. Thus in the so-called 'real world' it is present challenging what is thought to be impossible, and so edging us beyond political realism to imaginative political optimism. As I have said earlier the 'reserve' of the Easter gospel means that the Christian cannot be a Utopian in politics, that he is prepared to take a few modest steps in the right direction, but his belief that the 'forces of the age to come' are already at work in the world will not allow him to be imprisoned by the too modest expectations of those who pride themselves on being realists.

The whole issue of the Church and politics, which in recent years has become a matter of lively debate, is misrepresented as a clash between idealists and realists. In fact the fundamental bone of contention is what constitutes reality. The question which faith poses is: 'What is it to be a realist in a world where the one who stands for the ultimate value of persons was exposed to all that is stacked against the personal and yet was not crushed, where what is weak and ground down is shown to be the source of ultimate power?' The fact that Christ crucified is risen does not just mean that there are new spiritual possibilities, new thoughts and ideals around. Had Jesus cast aside his physicalness in his ascent to glory our expectations would then have been for transformed souls, but the empty tomb and the risen body forbid such a retreat into the purely 'spiritual'. In the fullness of his risen being, Christ knocks a hole through the ceiling of our too modest expectations. The mighty action of his cross and resurrection is an assault on the 'principalities and powers', on the determinism and fatalism which inhibit us from hoping too wildly (Col. 2:15).

We have been persuaded to accept our world as a closed world, shaped by the laws of nature or of the market, and by the realities of power politics. So the political task has seemed to be that of fitting humanity into this box. Jesus is the Jack in the Box, revealing the freedom of God to break through iron laws and do the impossible. He is the one who elicits the awe-struck question: 'Who then is this, that even wind and sea obey him?' (Mark 4:41). He is constantly urging his friends to have faith in a God for whom all things are possible: 'Whoever says to this mountain, "Be taken up and cast into the sea," and does not doubt in his heart, but believes that what he says will come to pass, it will be done for him' (Mark 11:23).

What we call 'miracle' is the sign that God's freedom is effective, not simply to change minds or to get individuals born again but to transform this material world. I find it significant that, when the Church looks for signs of sanctity in deciding whether a man or woman should be officially recognised as a saint, it still generally seeks evidence of miracles. In doing this an important point is being made. Christians are right to expect sanctity not to be wilting otherworldliness, but effective, a challenge to the way things are. A similar point is made in the insistence that the presence of the Lord in the Eucharist is real and with a reality that is not above or apart from the material bread and wine. We do not just eat and drink while our minds are stimulated to think about the Last Supper or to fashion some mental picture of Jesus of Nazareth. Material things are here the vehicle of his

123

presence. They have been transfigured to become 'the body and blood of Christ'.

The new creation makes a difference to things material, opens up for us fresh possibilities. 'Realists' in the past opposed the abolition of slavery and child labour on the grounds that such fine ideals were economically impossible, contrary to the laws of the market. Often it has proved to be the case, that what is called 'impossible' is simply what is undesirable for vested interests and that those who have dared to challenge such 'impossibilities' have succeeded in casting mountains into the sea.

Too good to be true?

Yet we hesitate. Are we not in danger of letting our imagination run away with our reason? Is it not too good to be true? Certainly at no point is it more difficult to test the truth claims of the Christian package for here those limitations of historical investigation which we noted earlier are most obvious. Ingenious though the arguments of Frank Morrison's famous book *Who Moved the Stone?* may be, they do not do justice to the fact that what meagre evidence we have comes not from detached observers but from plainly biased propagandists. The Easter stories are told to proclaim a faith in and commitment to this allegedly risen Christ. Furthermore if we have been right in representing the centre of the Easter gospel to be Jesus, in the fullness of his humanity passing into the glory of the Father, it is questionable what of this can be described as an event open to historical investigation. Certainly there is nothing to be observed in the passage of Jesus to the Father; however in the signs of assurance given to his friends it is different. Here something is said to have happened in time and space.

The allegation is that whatever happened involved a tomb once occupied by a corpse now being empty. In principle this tomb, if identifiable beyond reasonable doubt, could be investigated. If bones were found in it, which, again with a high degree of probability, could be identified as the bones of Jesus, say by showing marks of crucifixion and being of the right approximate dating, then this would count against the truthfulness of the resurrection as I have here represented it. Of course it would not dismay those whose Easter faith has already been detached from the body of Jesus but it would dismay me! But truth is truth and I would have to face the consequences. It was all a lovely dream but not in fact the case. However if the results of such hard-headed investigation could be decisive for unbelief's victory, they could never advance faith one inch. If the tomb was full, then the truth of the resurrection would be disproved; but if it was empty that truth would not thereby be proved. Alternative explanations for its emptiness would abound. The body could have been removed by pious disciples. It could have been stolen by a grave-robber.

In fact there is not much here for the historian to catch in his net. Whatever may be said of the 'empty tomb', Christ's rising is itself shrouded in mystery. But the historian can say things which are not without importance. He can say that Jesus died on the cross. He can say that, after a brief period, his followers erupted into an astonishingly vigorous life which was to have far-reaching results for the world. He would also have to record that these followers explained their new-found liveliness by claiming that this Jesus, who had certainly been dead, had come to life again and now, though hidden from sight, was closer to them than ever before. That of course would be recorded as the 'explanation' of committed followers. The historian would not, as historian, swallow it, but equally he could not swallow the ideological scepticism of those who require that it be ignored.

The inability of historical investigation to assist us much in the testing of the truth of Easter, leaves us with the greatest historical puzzle of all times. Dismiss the disciples' explanation of what happened as the mythological embroidery of fanatical religious sectarians, and you are still left to search for a plausible explanation of the astonishing success of a bunch of ordinary fishermen from a remote corner of the Roman Empire. Sit and listen to the Mozart Requiem or wander through the great cathedrals of Europe, sample just a little of the harvest which sprang from these men's sowing, and you cannot but wonder. Could all this really be the fruit of a delusion or cunning plot? Would fishermen be both crafty enough and foolish enough to concoct such an improbable tale and then suffer for their stubborn adherence to it? Is it plausible that the opponents of this sect, clearly anxious to scotch what they saw as a dangerous falsehood, failed to produce the decisive counter-evidence, the corpse of the crucified carpenter from the tomb? Although little hard fact is caught in the historian's net, a lot of hard questions are.

Of course whether we accept the apostolic answer or not will depend on factors other than those which the historian feels able to handle. It will depend on what we make of the life of Jesus which preceded his death and the life of his disciples which followed it. Assuredly something happened in between that dying and the liveliness of those friends which connects a man who once lived in Galilee with the movement which impinges upon us. The judgement we make about that 'something' will be governed by considerations of a more than historical nature. The great question is: do the presuppositions of the movement which says yes to the witness of the apostles, or those of the secular community which says no, make greater sense of the darkness, light and greyness which is the reality of human existence? Which rings true to life?

8

Called to the Dance

We have been standing on the river's edge testing the waters
for we cannot leap before we look. We dare not advance
beyond what integrity will allow. Christianity has, in theory,
although not always in practice, agreed with such caution.
Conscience, it has said, must always be followed. Yes, that
conscience must be informed, for it is no magical faculty
which can operate apart from reasonableness. We have no
warrant to speak boldly out of wilful ignorance. Yet at the
end of the day we have thoughtfully and honestly to follow
conscience. It is not only that we have nothing else to follow,
but that this insistence on personal integrity is required by
the very nature of God and of the relationship into which he
invites us. Love calls, love extends the offer of friendship and
there can be in love nothing of bullying or manipulation.

Our inevitable dependence on the tradition

So I am wary of issuing any peremptory summons to sign on
in the Christian army. My concern has been to make space
so that the seeker can edge forward without feeling jostled.
And yet I have tried to do this without cutting faith down to
what Jones can take. If his integrity is to be respected so too
must the integrity of the Christian Church.

We dare not offer anything less than we believe God to
have offered. But here we have to face a challenge to our
detached viewing, a disturbance of our position on the river
bank. Everything we have shown faith has to offer is inescapably offered through the strange package of the Christian
community. What lies before us is more than a book, however
holy, more than a series of dogmas, however essential.

Christianity, like its elder sister Judaism, is a religion of a people before that of a book. Of course the Holy Book is of supreme importance, articulating the tradition of faith which Jesus shared and his impact on that tradition. Of course dogmas are important as the signposts which keep a journeying people on the path of truth. But our concern has been not to sit still on a traditional foundation stone or simply gaze at signposts; it is to confront what has been built up from that foundation and to see where the paths of truth have led. We have wanted something more than an archaeological dig into Christian origins, to discover how a living community expresses itself in liturgies celebrated, prayers offered, justice struggled for, holy lives lived, pictures painted and music played. Although I have seemed to say nothing about the Church, in fact all that I have said is about it.

A casual theatregoer takes for granted the existence of a gulf between actors and audience. When he arrives, there is the stage mysteriously hidden by plush red curtains, and he can settle comfortably into his seat in the auditorium to munch his chocolates. As the curtain goes up, the division remains. Beyond the footlights are the godlike actors, while he is the passive spectator. But producers make great efforts to overcome this divide, to ease us out of our detached security and thrust us into the action. And this is no gimmick, for the truth is that there can be no dramatic communication without our involvement. The same is true of faith. To go back to our image of the river; we know that a point comes when we shall not get what we are after by remaining on the banks trying to fish out the bits of truth we fancy, but that we have to take the risk and jump into the river. If we still try to dodge the old boots and rubbish which we see floating on its waters, we have now made the discovery that it is only by allowing ourselves to be carried by its current that we shall reach our journey's end.

Taking the plunge

People become Christians by submitting to the rite of baptism which is precisely the enactment of being plunged into a river. The image has been somewhat blunted by the bowl of water taking the place of the running stream. It is now too easy to imagine that we are being enticed into a stagnant pool rather than a movement. 'Washing' has become the dominant theme. Certainly the 'washing away of evil' has its place in baptism (1 Pet. 3:21) but only in the context of the more violent image of taking the plunge, being submerged and coming up spluttering for breath, an image in fact of drowning and coming to life again. The old baptisteries at least made this clear. For instance in Ephesus you will be shown a small well with two sets of steps. Down one side the candidate for baptism would go, be plunged beneath the waters, and then come up the other side. That gets to the truth of the matter, the dying and coming to life again, the transition from the realm of darkness to the realm of light (1 Pet. 2:9). 'Do you not know that all of us who have been baptised into Christ Jesus were baptised into his death? We were buried therefore with him by baptism into death so that, as Christ was raised from the dead by the glory of the Father, we too might walk in newness of life' (Rom. 6:3–4).

The solidarity of sin and the solidarity of love

In fact these images of washing and drowning are connected. Becoming a Christian involves being removed from the solidarity of sin to the solidarity of love. In our earlier discussion we laid to one side consideration of 'original sin', that evil which we have not, as yet, deliberately chosen but which impinges upon and entices us. For good or ill, we are not isolated individuals but bound up with one another in the bundle of life.

If you look again at the cross as the place of judgement, the moment of truth, you will notice that, along with the deliberate choices which individuals make against Jesus, there is also an element of being dragged along, carried further into evil than these individuals, left to themselves, might have wanted to go. Simon Peter denies his master because he is edged into a corner. Pilate is seen as one drawn into the unjust condemnation of Jesus by political pressures. The crowd, shouting for the death penalty, appear victims of manipulation. Without in any way denying the freedom to say 'no' to such enticement, sin is a more complicated business than my personal wrong choices. So in the garden of Eden, before Adam and Eve say 'no' to the will of God, there is the enticing serpent, 'more subtle than any other wild creature', working away to blunt the edge of God's demand, the hidden persuader who dresses up darkness as light.

In Romans 7 St Paul shrewdly analyses the reality of this prevenient sin. In truth we are not as good as the ideals we hold. Our problem is not just that we do not know what we ought to do. Very often we know this only too clearly and still do not do it. Knowledge of the good does not ensure performance of the good:

> I do not do what I want, but I do the very thing I hate. Now if I do what I do not want, I agree that the law is good. So that it is no longer I that do it, but sin which dwells within me . . . For I do not do the good I want, but the evil I do not want is what I do. Now if I do what I do not want, it is no longer I that do it, but sin which dwells within me. (vv. 15–20)

It is this which makes the apostle describe our sinful condition as captivity or slavery. Far from being in a state of heady freedom liberated from the oppressive laws of God, I am in fact in bondage, deprived of my freedom to love: 'Wretched man that I am, who will deliver me from this body (this solidarity) of death?' (v. 24).

The answer is that rescue comes 'through Jesus Christ our lord' (v. 25). He rescues me, not only from my deliberately chosen sinfulness by his forgiveness, which refuses to allow my offence to become a barrier, but also from the solidarity of sin, 'the body of death', by transferring me to the new solidarity of his 'body'. It is in baptism that the vigorous biblical images of being rescued from Egypt, of being brought out of slavery or of being ransomed from captivity all come alive. By being plunged into this moving river I am carried from an environment where self is enthroned into one where love is enthroned in those signs and structures which entice me to live with Jesus the life that looks towards God. Here I begin to be set free to love, to enter into that glorious liberty of the children of God. Beneath the pressures of sin, which always remain in this life, I begin to recognise the greater pressure of divine grace, the enticement of that love which has proved stronger than sin and death. So the first purpose of baptism is this transference into the counter-culture of Christ's God-directed life: 'You were buried with him in baptism, in which you were raised with him' (Col. 2:12). Here we share, through prayer and sacrament, in Christ's Easter victory and begin to do the good which we know we ought to do. To the nature of this 'solidarity with Christ' we shall return as we try to grasp the depths of what Christians mean by 'communion' or fellowship.

The inescapable visible church

But we cannot go deeper by avoiding the flesh, by ignoring the visible and necessarily institutional human fellowship into which baptism brings us. In the gospels Jesus appears not as a solitary but as the leader of a band of followers. The real Jesus can never be separated from these friends. In contrast with the 'sinful body', they are called the 'body of Christ': 'We though many are one body in Christ and individually members one of another' (Rom. 12:5). While Jesus is said to be its 'head', 'we are members or limbs of that body' (Eph. 5:21ff). To be baptised is to become part of this one body (1 Cor. 12:13).

This exalted language is not used of some ideal church, 'the great church that is yet to be', but of the grubby and frequently scandalous Christian community of Corinth. It is important to grasp this for Christianity is inescapably about real people, in all their differences, divisiveness and sinfulness, thrown together in the workshop of Christ. Just as the differences of sex, race, colour and class cannot be used as a pretext for setting up a special church (Gal. 3:20), neither can the differences between the good, bad and indifferent. The community is, of its nature, universal, classless and unsectarian.

So it is impossible to be a lone Christian, an autonomous spiritual athelete scrabbling up a ladder far from the range of sinners. We are members one of another, living by the law of interdependence, learning to bear one another's burdens: 'If one member suffers, all suffer together; if one member is honoured, all rejoice together' (1 Cor. 12:26). Such common life means not only serving the needs of others but growing in that gracious charity which allows others to serve us, learning like Simon Peter that we have to permit the brother to wash our feet.

Indeed this learning to depend on others affects our understanding of and growth in the truth of Christ. Each of us has his or her own insights into this truth, yet we cannot set out to achieve a 'faith of our own' a do-it-yourself religion made up of such insights. At least if we do we shall end up with a lopsided and incomplete faith. We have to allow our brothers and sisters to wash our feet with truth, to learn precisely from those very bits of faith which seem to us most alien, least our 'cup of tea'. We need one another to be saved from the eccentricity of what von Balthasar has tersely called our 'own know-it-all wisdom'.

The New Testament is far from starry-eyed about the difficulties of life in community and gives a realistic picture of how easily human beings slip into jealousy, snobbery and party faction. Living with those we have not chosen is no simple matter. Naturally we gravitate towards the like-minded, to those who feel and think as we do. We are frankly more at home with our own inner circle of friends than in the give and take of community. Because the New Testament writers are fully aware of these difficulties they spend a good deal of time commending the sort of virtues which hold us together: 'Speak evil of no one, avoid quarrelling, be gentle, show perfect courtesy towards all men' (Tit. 3:2). Such down to earth and commonsense recipes for communal living are necessary in coping with the sometimes grim realities of church life. Yet it is St John who spells out the fundamental issue at stake by showing that the acceptance of one another in the community is the acid test of faith itself: 'If anyone says "I love God" and hates his brother, he is a liar; for he who does not love his brother whom he has seen, cannot love God whom he has not seen' (1 John 4:20).

The lure of the pure

For many, taking the plunge to become a Christian involves a hard struggle with a fastidiousness which shrinks from living cheek by jowl with this particular group of mediocre, mixed up and boring people. It is not that they are too good to be true, too spiritual, too earnest, but apparently so half-hearted, so evidently embroiled in the petty appurtenances of church life and the little power games of any small group. Those who are sensitive to the mystery of God and the deep seriousness of faith are repelled. Instead of joining this lot whose eyes seem more firmly set on the next jumble sale than on the kingdom of God, give us a few picked souls in a group for study or prayer and then we can get down to business. It is all very well for the naturally gregarious who can savour such human oddities and find much in them to chuckle over, but for the shy and reserved the all too human outer shell of faith is a real burden.

I have known good and godly people for whom the greeting of peace at the Eucharist has become a moment of sheer agony. As they shy away from such tokens of warm fellowship, they are not less loving than their neighbours but often painfully aware of the difficulties of genuine love and cannot bear to see this precious thing reduced to mere genial goodwill. I once presided over an Anglican church where, although many came to a truly friendly and welcoming parish Eucharist, a minority chose to slip in and out of a quiet early morning Eucharist or a weekday evensong. They could easily be dismissed as stand-offish or unwilling to accept the claims of Christian fellowship, and yet, as I came slowly to know them, and it was slow because they were an elusive bunch, I discovered in their ranks some who spent their working hours giving out love in demanding and caring jobs. I have known many delightful outgoing priests who possess the precious gift of being able to put others at their ease, but I also know that, when I have wanted to be listened to in a way in which deep and difficult things could be allowed to surface, it has often been to shy and withdrawn pastors that I have turned. For Christians fellowship is inescapable but it is too often confused with jollity. Real loving, rather than holding us in a too-warm embrace, is able to be quiet, to listen and catch the unspoken cry which comes from the heart. Love does not smother but sets us free to be ourselves.

The breadth and depth of community

The New Testament never rests content with that superficial good cheer which sails under the flag of 'Christian fellowship'. It points us rather to the hidden breadth of the community, assuring us that Tom, Dick and Harry next to us in the pew are but the tip of an iceberg, that to enter Christian fellowship is to know that we have 'come to Mount Zion and to the city of the living God, the heavenly Jerusalem; and the inumerable angels in festal gathering, to the assembly of the firstborn who are enrolled in heaven; and to a judge who is God of all, to the spirits of just men made perfect' (Heb. 12:22–23). What we see around us is but a tiny part of that vast concourse, the communion of saints. In praying for the dead, in asking for the prayers of the saints and in being conscious that in our worship we are joined with angels and archangels and the whole company of heaven, the true dimensions of Christian fellowship are discovered. Without this sense of perspective our worship becomes claustrophobic and our service a lonely grind.

But if faith points thus to the breadth of community, it also points to its depths. This vast human community of the living and the dead, this workshop of giving and receiving in love, is but a sacrament of divine fellowship: 'That which we have seen and heard we proclaim also to you, so that you may have fellowship with us and our fellowship is with the Father and with his Son Jesus Christ' (1 John 1:3). Friendship with one another and friendship with God are thus bound together. The common life of Christians leads on to the common life we are to share with God. That is why baptism is always more than becoming a member of a community; it is first and foremost a plunging into the life of Christ.

We rightly read John 17 as the manifesto of Christian unity. The prayer of Jesus is 'that they may all be one' (v. 21) and there is no escape from the demand that this unity be real, visible and institutional. But this embodiment of unity, what used to be called 'organic unity', matters, not for the sake of making Christianity in some imperial and thus impressive model, but as an expression, an incarnation, of the unity which exists between Jesus and the one he calls Father. The disciples are to be one 'even as thou Father art in me and I in thee, that they also may be in us ... that they may be one even as we are one, I in them and thou in me, that they may become perfectly one' (vv. 22–23). The fellowship of the friends of Jesus is to be rooted and grounded in the fellowship of Father and Son in the Holy Spirit. Christian 'communion' is always deficient unless it points to divine 'communion'.

Divine communion revealed

When St Mark announces 'the beginning of the gospel of Jesus Christ the Son of God', he starts, not with stories of the birth of Jesus, but abruptly with his baptism at the hands of John in the river Jordan. This event spotlights the solidarity of Jesus both with humanity and God. He who is the Son of God does not stand aloof from the human condition but is 'made to be sin who knew no sin, so that in him we might become the righteousness of God' (2 Cor. 5:21). Thus he takes his place in the queue of penitents and, plunging into the river with us sinners, submits to the baptism of repentance. There he sets his course on that journey which is to take him right down into the depths of our lostness, reaching its climax on Calvary and his entry into the place of the dead.

Here too his solidarity with God is revealed. The drama of the baptism is the drama of divine as well as human solidarity. There Jesus stands in the river. There is the vision of the Spirit 'descending upon him like a dove'. There is the voice which comes from heaven saying, 'Thou art my beloved Son'. Which part of the picture, we ask, represents the mystery of God, the man, the dove or the voice? The answer has to be that the mystery is in all three, that the mystery revealed is precisely the interaction between the three. God is glimpsed in the outpourer of love, in the recipient of love and in the communicator of love. This event is the overture to Christ's mission, encapsulating themes later to be developed. 'I have a baptism to be baptised with; and how I am constrained until it is accomplished' (Luke 12:50). The real baptism, for which what happened in Jordan was but a rehearsal, took place on Calvary where the divine interaction reaches its climax, with Jesus, who has received all from the Father, now handing back that all to the Father: 'Father into thy hand I commit my spirit' (Luke 23:46).

In the light of the Jordan disclosure of this divine interaction we begin to see the life of Jesus as something more than the solo flight of a religious genius. If the gospels are reticent about his inner life, they do speak clearly of his consciousness of being a partner in this interaction. See how at once Mark shows Jesus propelled from the Jordan by the communicator of love: 'the Spirit immediately drove him out into the wilderness' (Mark 1:12). See how he remains always linked to the Father in prayer: 'In the morning, a great while before day, he rose and went out to a lonely place and there he prayed' (Mark 1:35).

The gospels are consistent in painting a portrait of Jesus which is simultaneously one of great power, mystery and authority and of self-effacement. The one who elicits the awed question 'who is this?' yet always lives to point beyond himself to the Father. At first sight this combination seems undermined in the fourth gospel with the Son's ringing claims: 'I am the resurrection and the life' (John 11:25); 'I am the way, and the truth and the life . . . he who has seen me has seen the Father' (John 14:6,9). What place is there here for self-effacement? Yet in fact no other gospel makes so explicit the Son's total dependence on the Father. He is the one who has come down from heaven, not to do his own will but the will of him who sent him (6:38); 'My teaching is not my own but his who sent me. . . He who speaks on his own authority seeks his own glory; but he who seeks the glory of him who sent him is true' (7:16,18). Everything Jesus holds has been lavished on him as gift from the Father: 'He whom God has sent utters the words of God, for it is not by measure that he gives the Spirit. The Father loves the Son and has given all things into his hand' (3:34,35). The Son's task, his life's work, is to hand all this back, to return total love with total love, which is at the same time a handing of himself over in love to us.

136

God is love – interdependence in the life of God

Christians believe they have glimpsed God in Jesus who is not solitary, but always in solidarity with the Father in the bond of the Holy Spirit. The mystery which is not dispelled is no longer 'faceless'; we now dare to say that astounding thing 'God is love' (1 John 4:8). That statement is often thought to be 'simple' religion in contrast to the unnecessary complications of dogma, yet in truth it is the complex thing to which dogma, in halting and always inadequate words, seeks to bear witness. In saying 'God is love' we are saying something more than 'God loves us', we are claiming that he IS love before there was any 'us' to be loved. Within God there is the completeness of love so that he did not need a world to become capable of love. God is, as we should say, 'fulfilled' containing within himself not only love to give but the other to receive that love. The drama of the divine interaction focused at Jordan and worked out in that giving and receiving of love which is the secret of the life of Jesus, shows what is true for ever about the mystery of God. This joyful interdependence is what the life of God is.

Holy Trinity – the picture and the dogma

In talking thus we are talking about God as Holy Trinity. 'Now the catholic faith is this . . . that we worship one God in Trinity and the Trinity in unity – neither confounding the persons nor dividing the substance.' So runs an old credal hymn, the Athanasian creed. The language is abstract and quite unlike the vivid picture of Christ's baptism in the Jordan. Such language is best used as the art critic's comments on a picture; they can illuminate but are no substitute for the picture itself. Trinitarian dogma is thus not a formula encasing some esoteric ideology but an encouragement to look ever more carefully at the original picture, to pay attention to what we may only have glanced at. Alas, school children are often bored to tears by the classroom analysis of a Shakespeare play, for, taken to pieces before their eyes, the drama seems to be lost. Indeed of all literary forms, commentaries seem often the most deadly, leaving us

137

lost in a detailed examination of tree trunks and deprived of any view of the wood. But such dissection can bring deeper understanding. The exercise is shown to be worthwhile when we are able to return to a reading or enactment of the drama with eyes more open and ears more alert.

The same is true of the dogma of God as Holy Trinity. 'There is one person of the Father, another of the Son, another of the Holy Ghost.' This insistence on the integrity or uniqueness of the divine 'persons' only makes sense when we return to the New Testament portrait. In the dialogue between Jesus and his Father we see that love does not involve a loss of identity, the merging of personality in some divine collective, but on the contrary the fulfilment, the enhancement of identity. So Jesus does not appear as a puppet manipulated by some force beyond him but gloriously free to be himself. It is precisely in his unceasing obedience to the Father that he finds perfect freedom. So for us obedience is rescued from sterile conformism, and freedom rescued from a search for selfish autonomy. Moreover, although we speak of the three 'persons' of the Trinity, we do not have here a hierarchy of gods, with the Father at the top of the scale and the Son at the bottom. 'In this Trinity', the dogma insists, 'there is no before or after, no greater or less. But all three persons are co-eternal together and co-equal.' The freedom of the 'persons' to be themselves in diversity is not in conflict with their fundamental equality of status. Thus Jesus, wholly dependent on the Father and wholly obedient to his will, yet speaks to him with that unique boldness, '*Abba* – Daddy', and unselfconsciously exercises his authority, 'Son, be of good cheer, your sins are forgiven'; 'if it is by the finger of God that I cast out demons, then the kingdom of God has come upon you' (Luke 11:20). For the three characters of the baptismal scene, the man, the dove, the voice, represent not three gods but one, the one God who was in Christ reconciling the world to himself.

The dogma of the Trinity does not undermine the divine unity. Here one has to admit that the use of the word 'person' can be highly misleading. The Latin 'persona' does not have its modern connotation of an individual centre of consciousness. It is always the one which has a share in some common property. 'Persona' used in a modern context inevitably seems to suggest that the threefoldness of God involves a committee of gods. And yet to replace it, as Karl Barth does with 'mode of being', and thus to speak of Father, Son and Holy Spirit as three 'modes' of the one divine being, although done by him with great caution and with the deliberate intention of distancing himself from the early heresy of 'modalism', misses something of the revolution which is wrought in our understanding of the nature of divine unity. As the nineteenth-century Anglican theologian F. D. Maurice showed, the question is: what sort of unity is the unity of God? His answer is that, in the light of Christ, it must be 'no bare mathematical unity', but a unity capable of embracing diversity.

Far from it being recondite mystification, the dogma is simply articulating what it means to say 'God is love' and in so doing connects with the experience of those created in the image and likeness of this God. In our deepest human relationships we discover that true equality of persons, far from destroying individuality, enhances it. To fall in love is to discover both equality and freedom. In the impersonal relationships of society the battle rages between equality and freedom. But even here we glimpse the possibility of reconciliation through that third person of the secular trinity, fraternity. We see that, in our uniqueness, we yet belong together and have therefore to use this precious uniqueness for the common good and not for divisive self-agrandisement. 'You were called to freedom, brethren; only do not use your freedom as an opportunity for the flesh, but through love be servants of one another' (Gal. 5:13).

Practical Christianity – being caught up in love

What a step we have taken from the grubby realities of Christian communities to the splendour of the divine Trinity! Yet the purpose of the former is that we might share in a fellowship which reaches through and beyond human fellowship right into that fellowship which is 'with the Father and his Son Jesus Christ'. In making what seems an esoteric movement from the depths to the heights, plain 'practical Christianity' is vindicated. Those who say the religion of Jesus is not a doctrine but a 'way of life' are ultimately right. Nothing matters more than loving. Where your 'plain' Christian is often wrong is in his superficial understanding of what such loving might involve and his reduction of the 'way of life' to obeying a code of conduct.

The second Epistle of Peter challenges such a pedestrian view when it insists that we are to become nothing less than 'partakers of the divine nature' (2 Pet. 1:4). St Paul similarly moves us away from programmes for self-improvement when he insists that the love to which we are called is gift before it is task: 'God's love has been poured into our hearts through the Holy Spirit which has been given to us' (Rom. 5:5). The same Spirit who descends like a dove on Jesus at his baptism and from all eternity binds together Father and Son in mutual love and self-giving, is now given to us. In his letter to the Galatians the apostle presents the divine life in the image of a family circle of love with Jesus as the true son and heir. Our fulfilment lies in being adopted into this family circle, becoming sons and daughters by his gracious action (Gal. 4). The Holy Spirit is for us 'the spirit of adoption' so that:

> all who are led by the Spirit of God are sons of God. For you did not receive the spirit of slavery to fall back into fear, but you have received the Spirit of sonship. When we cry 'Abba, Father', it is the Spirit himself bearing witness with our spirit that we are children of God, and if children then heirs, heirs of God and fellow heirs with Christ. (Rom. 8:14–17)

Of course such talk of the divine 'family circle' is but a picture, but it does get across something of the richness of love's interaction in eternal giving and receiving and our calling to become involved in it. I am particularly fond of the medieval image of the 'dance', in which Jesus is seen as the divine dancer taking the floor to dance out the figure of God's love. All this he does for our sake, 'to call his true love to the dance'. In his living and dying that pattern of the divine dance is revealed so that we wallflowers, his true love, might accept his invitation to take the floor and be caught up in that dance.

Seen like this the trinitarian vision of God is not abstruse theory for advanced believers but the simple centre of practical religion. If we would, with whatever hesitations, step out on the path of love, we do so in the knowledge that love is not something we can generate by our efforts, not a matter of grim determination to obey a rule, but first something which is there before we were there, that which is most real, most basic to the universe, the 'love which moves the sun and other stars' (Dante, *Paradiso*, 33.145). Practical religion thus centres not on anxious attempts at self-improvement, but on looking outwards to rejoice that this love is there. To gaze at the love which is beyond us yet undergirds and summons us, is to look at reality, at ultimate truth. This is what believers are after when they affirm the primacy of worship and adoration.

The two loves united

I am conscious in this work of continually jumping between the heights and the depths – of saying a word now about prayer and now about politics, of facing some of the distasteful things about ecclesiastical life and then leaping away to point to the divine Trinity. As I leap I overhear the voices of my readers, one complaining, 'Just as he is getting down to earth he becomes dreamy and mystical'; another, 'Just as we move towards prayer and the sublime heights of faith, he will keep dragging in politics.'

I make no apologies. How could it be possible for a faith which discerns the holy in the homely to tolerate any division between worldliness and otherworldliness? How could we be left to agonise over whether we have poured out too much love on the creature and not kept back enough for God when the way of the Word made flesh is simultaneously that of solidarity with humanity and with the divine mystery? Jesus can love the Father with his whole being and his neighbour as himself because in God there is no either/or, no careful balance to be maintained, for God is love. To pursue with Jesus this God is inevitably to be driven into the depths of human need. To be caught up in his love which moves boldly on to the Father is to be caught up in the same love which moves ever outwards to the furthest corners of the earth. Our fulfilment as human beings cannot be other than that of the pioneer of faith, to come home to the mystery of God and to be set free to love our neighbour. So politics without prayer and prayer without politics are equally deadly. They pull apart what God in Christ has bound together.

Trinitarian faith and prayer

The obvious connecting point between the two loves is the prayer of intercession, asking God for things for other people. In a religion of bearing one another's burdens such prayer must have a high priority. How too could it be otherwise when the Lord taught us to pray not 'my' but 'our' Father, to ask not for my own but for 'our' daily bread?

And yet asking God to feed the hungry, heal the sick, to give justice and peace looks suspiciously like trying to persuade him to do something he would not otherwise do, while at the same time very conveniently getting ourselves off the hook. Intercession seems to involve an attempt to manipulate God and evade our own responsibility. Some who seek to avoid this danger transform intercession into a therapy for making ourselves more sensitive to the cares and needs of the world. Instead of trying to persuade God to do something, it is said, we are really persuading ourselves, softening our hard hearts and thus preparing for a more energetic commitment to human responsibilities. Certainly serious prayer must lead to the acceptance not evasion of responsibility. The reality of our prayer for the starving of Ethiopia is tested, not by its passion but by our readiness to do the little we can by giving money and, in a democracy, persuading governments to be both generous and wise. However I do not believe that intercession can be reduced to self-persuasion nor that what it has traditionally meant necessarily involves an attempt to manipulate God. The starting point for faith has to be the recognition that God's care and concern for those we pray for exceeds our own. He does not have to be persuaded to love for he loves more than we do and with a farsightedness we could never achieve: 'If you then who are evil know how to give good gifts to your children, how much more will your

Father who is in heaven give good things to those who ask him?' (Matt. 7:11).

Of course God knows what we want before we ask (Matt. 6:32) and yet Jesus insists that he still requires us to ask (Matt. 7:7). Why is this? Partly because the Father wants his children to come before him as they are, thus ready to speak their minds and ask for what their hearts desire. But beyond that, it is because this God of love cannot work by the sort of magic that disposes of our human free will and cooperation. He cannot do other than involve us, catch us up in the dance of his mighty actions.

It is this relationship between God's actions and ours which lies at the heart of the doctrine of the virginal conception of Jesus and indeed of all honouring of the mother of the Lord. The story of the angel coming to Mary clearly requires us to see the coming of the Saviour as the divine gift, the result of God's initiative. It is not the case that human wisdom or goodness had reached such a peak that Jesus had, as it were, evolved from it. He comes 'not of blood, nor of the will of the flesh nor of the will of man' (John 1:13) but of God. Thus Joseph stands helplessly to one side allowing the power of the Most High to overshadow Mary, that same power which hovered over the primeval chaos to bring about the first creation, now effecting the new Creation. Mary is 'full of grace', primarily because she has been called and has found favour with God (Luke 1:30) and is thus the recipient of God's gift. But because of this she is also 'graceful', with a life open to and fashioned by the divine activity. If the priority lies with God's initiative and action, yet, as the love which woos and does not crush, he must courteously await Mary's free 'yes', 'be it unto me according to thy will', which signals active human cooperation rather than mere resignation. Like St Paul (1 Cor. 3:9) Mary really is a 'fellow worker' with God. The overwhelmingness of divine grace does not act as a bulldozer reducing to rubble the significance of human action.

It is this relationship between divine and human love which must control our understanding of prayer. To intercede for others is not to try to persuade an otherwise indifferent God to act but, in this particular situation and for this particular

143

person, to add our 'yes' of active cooperation to the loving will of God. In performing this free action we are adding to the sum total of human response to the divine mystery. The world as it is holds back this 'yes', slams the door in his face; and because love remains steadfast and declines to force our freedom, the world's refusal must also hold back the doing of love's will. So in Mark's gospel we read that at Nazareth Jesus was not able to do any mighty works because of the unbelief of his fellow townsfolk (Mark 6:5).

Our faith, this response which is genuinely 'ours', does not of course manufacture the answer which we seek to our prayer. We are not suggesting, as some forms of Christian healing do with their insistence that the 'harder' we pray the more likely it is that the sick will recover, that our faith creates the healing love of God. Just as in the Eucharist faith does not 'make' the presence of Christ but welcomes the Lord who comes so that his coming might be fruitful in us, so in our intercession we open the door to allow the creative love of God to be set free in our world. In this sense, it is certainly the case that the 'more' prayer there is the better.

Because, as we have said, our prayer commits us to further cooperation with God's love, doing what is in our power to do, there is truth in the words, 'he has no hands but our hands'; however the cooperation of prayer, this 'yes' to the will of God, is valid in its own right and not simply as a springboard for further action. Such is the fundamental need of the world for openness to God and such is our human interdependence, that the cooperation with God through prayer of a contemplative nun in her convent or a house-bound invalid in Manchester can have an incalculable effect throughout the world. We do not have to be on the spot to open the door to the loving action of God.

All our praying has to centre on the recognition that God's love is greater than our own, that while our love is flagging, often foolish and shortsighted, his is consistent, wise and capable of seeing the whole picture. Certainly our prayer should be natural and specific. If a friend had cancer it would be highly artificial to pray that he acquired the gift of patience, and not to pray for his recovery. Seeing the starving children of Mozambique, who would pray for an increase of missionaries rather than an increase of grain? Yet, as we recognise the littleness and blindness of our love, we can genuinely come to share the prayer of Jesus, 'nevertheless not my will, but thine'. Far from persuading God to be as caring as we are, what are we doing but emptying our little buckets of love into the ocean of his love, conscious that what we have in our buckets has been drawn from that same ocean? All this is to speak out of our trinitarian vision of God, recognising that we do not manufacture a love of our own but are caught up in the dance of love, adopted into the family circle of divine charity. The act of emptying my bucket into the ocean matters because it is through my act of freedom that his love is to be set free; but to change the image, while I may open the door it is the love beyond which comes flooding in.

Prayer which is gift before it is labour

The recognition of this pre-existing love is the foundation stone of all prayer. As I have insisted much of our prayer is a fitful distracted business, a struggle to make what Cardinal Hume has called the 'prayer of incompetence'. It is of course important that we persevere but equally that we do not try to force ourselves into what we imagine to be a more 'pious' frame of mind. When we most energetically struggle against distractions, we find ourselves ever more enmeshed in them.

There are many for whom prayer has become a joyless grind, the shouldering of a burden of guilt and failure. To such every book or sermon on prayer only accentuates the gulf between their poor efforts and what they take to be 'real' prayer. What is needed is the ability to relax and so rediscover the truth that prayer is God's activity before it is our task. Before I start praying, prayer is there, that movement of love ever carried on between Father and Son in the bond of Holy Spirit, that divine friendship which has been there from all eternity. All the time the clue has been to hand in the over-familiar formula which we have tagged on to our prayers 'through Jesus Christ our Lord'. So to pray is to be seized by the 'spirit of adoption', that very Spirit 'who searches the hearts of men' (Rom. 8:27) and 'intercedes for us with sighs too deep for words' (Rom. 8:26); and so to be given a share in the prayer which Jesus makes, '*Abba*, Father . . . thy will be done'. Instead of labouring to manufacture 'my own prayer life' I receive Christ's as a gift, I am plunged into the divine relationship of love.

The seeker sought

Just as prayer is reborn when we discover it as gift, so our whole pilgrimage towards God may be seen in a new light when we make the same discovery. We have bbeen gazing at this strange Christian thing, which stands before us, trying to give our attention to a complex and sometimes maddening picture. Much is puzzling, much dull and meaningless, much even repulsive, and yet we have glimpsed some shafts of light, felt that this funny old thing, whatever its manifest faults, does justice to the heights and depths of human existence, at least takes seriously some of our real questions.

In our cottage garden are two old apple trees. They are covered with wart-like growths, they rock perilously in any gale and sometimes fail to produce much fruit. The cry goes up: 'Chop them down. Let them make way for new trees.' But they remain, for they are very beautiful and again and again surprise us with rich crops. There is much that is truly awful in the Christian thing, much cruelty and pride masquerading as godly zeal, much insensitivity to human need and much evasion of truth, and yet among the grottiness we have glimpsed the gold. Somehow here is the hook which fits the eye of my deepest experience of life. Of course the puzzles have not ended nor the questions ceased. If I am on the right path, I shall yet find myself crying with Catherine of Siena: 'Eternal Trinity, you are like a deep sea, in which the more I seek, the more I find, and the more I find, the more I seek' (*On Divine Revelation*).

All I can do is to edge forward with what light I have been given, refusing to be hustled by others or to settle down in some comfortable niche fashioned of my 'bright' ideas. Maybe the moment comes when I can honestly say something like this: 'Mystery of divine truth, I want to believe all that truth which you have shown of yourself. Lord, I believe, help thou my unbelief.' And this perhaps is the moment when I discover that faith, like prayer, is ultimately a gift, something to be received and not manufactured. It is the moment when I sense the solid 'thereness' of God, the presence of mystery which goes before and surrounds my every pilgrim step. Looking back over the road I have travelled so far, I notice something more than my own faintly comic questioning and struggling, the presence of a stranger who has been questioning me, struggling with me. I am Jacob wrestling with the stranger until the break of day, the one to whom I have cried: 'I will not let you go unless you bless me'; the one whom I discover to be the very mystery I have sought (Gen. 32:24ff).

That little bit of faith I have got I have not achieved but received. The God I thought I had discovered has discovered me. The real drama was not my wrestling with God, but his with me. I have been pursued and hunted down by him. However much I may have wanted him, he has wanted me more.